DANIEL CRAIG

THIS IS A CARLTON BOOK

This edition published in 2013 by Carlton Books Limited
20 Mortimer Street
London W1T 3JW

First published in 2009

10 9 8 7 6 5 4 3 2 1

Text and design copyright © Carlton Books Limited 2009, 2013

The right of Tina Ogle to be identified as the author of this work
has been asserted by her in accordance with the Copyright,
Designs and Patents Act 1988.

A CIP catalogue record for this book is available from the
British Library.

ISBN 978-1-78097-407-1

Printed in Dubai

DANIEL CRAIG

THE ILLUSTRATED BIOGRAPHY

TINA OGLE

CARLTON BOOKS

CONTENTS

INTRODUCTION

When aspiring actor Daniel Craig was growing up in the Wirral he
could never have dreamed that a picture of him wearing clinging blue
swimming trunks would one day flash around the world, inspiring
undisguised lust in every woman who saw it.

Having announced his intentions to be an actor at the age of six, he should have been preparing himself for the limelight and the adulation of adoring fans. But years later as a struggling young actor it seemed that it was interesting work, albeit work that paid the bills, that he craved rather than notoriety or sex symbol status.

Having haunted Liverpool's Everyman Theatre with his mother as a child, hanging out with the actors backstage as well as watching the productions, he saw acting as a life he fancied for himself. Never particularly academically minded, he left school without qualifications and won a place on a National Youth Theatre scheme in London. Moving to the big, bad capital city on his own at the age of seventeen, he did his fair share of menial jobs to get by, though he is keen to point out that he was 'no Dick Whittington'. His ambition burned long and bright as it took him many attempts and several years to get into drama school, his persistence eventually paying off with a place at the prestigious Guildhall School of Music and Drama.

His peers at Guildhall included many now famous names such as Rhys Ifans, Ewan McGregor and Alastair McGowan. He seemed unimpressed with his three years there though, commenting casually that it had at least taught him not to shout backstage. Graduating in 1991, he then began the grind of becoming recognised and getting his name and face known in theatre and TV. He was lucky enough to be cast in a film before he left drama school, playing a bullying Afrikaans cop in *The Power Of One*, but this was not to be a breakthrough role.

Small roles in TV series such as *Boon* and *Drop The Dead Donkey* as well as more interesting theatre jobs supplemented his income while working in bars and restaurant kitchens. And then along came *Our Friends In The North* in 1996. This state-of-the-nation BBC drama serial with a plot spanning more than two decades was to bring him to national attention in the most positive way.

Playing Geordie Peacock, a Newcastle lad who dreamed of becoming a pop star but was forced to flee his violent father, Daniel shone. His portrayal of the essentially decent man who ends up working for a porn boss in London's Soho, then descends to living on the streets and being flung into prison, won him a legion of new fans. Along with his role as Jemmy Seagrove opposite Alex Kingston in that year's ITV drama *Moll Flanders*, it seemed that he would be the nation's favourite new bit of Northern 'rough'.

But Daniel was having none of it, deeply regretting an interview he'd given to a woman's magazine about eligible bachelors. He shied away from any suggestion that he become a sex symbol and the darling of the lifestyle press.

It was a brave decision at the time. A heightened profile and women slavering over him would undoubtedly have led to more work. But he wanted to succeed on the strength of his acting rather than on his looks. So he eschewed the chance to be flavour of the month in the hope that

Opposite: Daniel steals a kiss from Saskia Wickham in ITV's *Boon* in 1992.
Below: Daniel played a burglar who became Francis Bacon's lover in the 1998 movie *Love is the Devil*.

building up a decent body of work would pay off more handsomely in the end.

Other rather forgettable TV roles followed as well as a well-received turn in a play at the Old Vic. And he started to make interesting independent movies, the most notable of which was *Love Is The Devil*, a biopic of Francis Bacon. He played Bacon's, burglar lover, a role that hardly made him housewives' choice, but simulating S&M with Derek Jacobi didn't bother him in the least. In the same year, he played a killer in period piece *Elizabeth*, and it was this that was to catch Bond producer Barbara Broccoli's eye. That

wasn't to pay off in terms of casting until some seven years later, but it showed that Daniel was making the right choices in terms both of being seen and in having his talent recognised.

He veered from the independent mode sharply in 2001 with a role in *Lara Croft: Tomb Raider* alongside Angelina Jolie. Admitting afterward that he took a risk in order to raise his profile, he was deeply unhappy with the resulting film and his role in it. He even pretended to stab himself in an interview with a journalist when he found out that revered critic Tom Paulin had been forced to watch it for a reviews programme.

While not a shining star on his CV, *Tomb Raider* did him no lasting damage. The very next year he was cast in Sam Mendes' bleak period gangster movie *Road To Perdition*, playing Hollywood legend Paul Newman's son. A big-budget Hollywood movie with style and class, this was much more up his street. But still Hollywood wasn't beating down his door and he admitted that he wasn't keen on pushing himself to hustle for work in America.

Nonetheless, high quality British movies followed with *The Mother*, Sylvia Plath biopic *Sylvia*, *Enduring Love* and *Layer Cake*. While by no means making him a household name, he was increasingly

Above: Alex Kingston shared some raunchy sex scenes with Daniel in the ITV drama *Moll Flanders.*

Right: Daniel played a man with no name, simply billed as 'XXXX' in *Layer Cake.*

being noticed by the people that mattered. In 2005, Steven Spielberg cast him in *Munich*, his controversial film about the events following the slaying of Israeli athletes at the 1972 Olympic Games.

Also in 2005 came the momentous announcement that he would be taking over as James Bond.

Rumours had been circulating for a while that he would be the first blond Bond. When it was confirmed in October 2005, his casting was greeted with howls of outrage from the popular press and from many amongst the legions of dedicated Bond fans.

Dismissed as too ugly, too blond, too short and too common to play the nation's favourite spy, Daniel admitted to having a few dark hours as he absorbed the criticism. The tabloid press were perhaps hoping to rattle him into some kind of angry reaction. His relationship with the press had never been an easy one. He'd likened self promotion to going to the dentist and hadn't been best pleased when his brief relationship with supermodel Kate Moss was splashed all over the papers. To his credit, Daniel kept his head down, gritted his teeth and got on with it. Months in the gym paid off with the physique that had females all over the world swooning and he battled bravely through injuries to do as much as possible of the demanding stunt work himself on his debut Bond film *Casino Royale*.

He must have permitted himself more than one small smile when the film opened to rave reviews and fantastic box office takings in November 2006. Further cementing his Bond credentials with *Quantum Of Solace* in 2008, and continuing to mix quirky, independent movies with big screen blockbusters, his career continues apace.

As someone who tried so hard early on to avoid the 'sex symbol' tag, Daniel is sure to be embarrassed by the fact that you can buy a replica pair of those famous trunks on the Internet. But has he managed to make the role of James Bond his own, keep his independence and prove the carping critics spectacularly wrong.

For those reasons, he deserves our admiration and our respect.

Above: Even the most ruthless 'Bond' ever to hit the screen was able to display some tender moments.

HOYLAKE C OF E
PRIMARY SCHOOL
HOYLAKE
1979
CLASS 10

1

EARLY LIFE

When Daniel Wroughton Craig was born on 2 March, 1968 in Chester

in the north west of England, it must have seemed very unlikely to his

parents that their tiny son would one day be James Bond. Swaggering

Scottish actor Sean Connery occupied the world's most famous tuxedo

at that time, having wowed audiences in *Dr No*, *From Russia With Love*,

Goldfinger, *Thunderball* and the previous year's *You Only Live Twice*.

D aniel's mother, Carol Olivia, an art teacher, may well have harboured thespian ambitions for him. She herself had had to turn down a place at RADA to pursue a more practical career in teaching. His dad, Tim, a former merchant seaman and steel erector who eventually became a pub landlord, was just happy to have a healthy son. Daniel joined his older sister, Lea, to swell the ranks of the Craig family at 41 Liverpool Road, Chester.

The happy family unit wasn't destined to last though, as Craig's parents split up when he was four and his mother took him and his sister to live in central Liverpool. They remained here until he was nine when they moved to nearby Hoylake on the west coast of the Wirral. It sounded pretty idyllic as Craig later described it: 'On the beach, near where they got Red Rum fit again, where the sand goes out for miles.' Every child loves to romp around on a beach and if the seaside near his home was good enough for Red Rum, three times winner of the Grand National, it was certainly good enough for an energetic kid with dreams of appearing on the big screen.

Despite his parents' divorce, it seems that Daniel had a stable and happy childhood, maintaining regular contact with his dad, as he does to this day. He also has a close relationship with his step dad, artist Max Blond, whom Carol later married.

Daniel's mother followed her love of drama through regular trips to the famous Everyman Theatre in Liverpool, where she was friendly with many of the actors. At this time, the group included the now famous comic actress Julie Walters; Bernard Hill, who shone in Alan

Previous spread: A young Daniel Craig with classmates at Hoylake Primary School in 1979.
Below: Daniel's mother took him on regular trips to the famous Everyman Theatre in Liverpool.

Bleasdale's *Boys From The Blackstuff*, and renowned playwright Willy Russell. Her children accompanied her on these ventures and the atmosphere had a lasting impact on young Daniel.

'I guess I got into acting because I liked showing off,' he told *Arena* magazine in 2006. 'When we lived in Liverpool my mother had friends in the theatre and me and my sister spent a lot of time there. I got the bug, it was as simple as that. I'd see the plays or I would be in the lighting box backstage and I knew that was what I wanted to do.'

He also stunned his dad on a visit to his Ring O' Bells pub in Frodsham near Chester when he announced his ambitions at the age of six. As Tim Wroughton-Craig recalls: 'I remember having some musician friends over and little Daniel was weaving in and out of their legs. One asked him what he was going to do when he grew up and without breaking stride he said "be an actor". I remember at the time blinking and doing a double-take because he said it with such certainty and he was so small.'

Daniel wasted no time in pursuing his ambition. On a holiday with his maternal

Above: Daniel aged 15 appearing in the Heswall Woolgatherers Amateur Dramatic Society's production of Alan Bleasdale's *Sitting on the Old School Bench*.

Above: Daniel (centre with striped tie) again with his fellow thespians of the Heswall Woolgatherers.

grandparents, Olwyn and Doris Williams, at the age of eight, he devised, wrote and staged a show on a cruise in the Norwegian fjords. What the early critical reception was for the budding impresario is not recorded. As his mother Carol later told the local paper: 'It was all he ever wanted to do and I was somehow always quite sure he was going to make it. He was always performing.'

He has described his childhood as being both very happy and very ordinary, telling his good friend, artist Sam Taylor-Wood, in an interview in *Interview* magazine: 'I lived just outside Liverpool with my mother and my sister. At the time, my life probably seemed quite extraordinary, but actually it was very ordinary. I went through school, failed my Eleven Plus exams, went to a secondary school with little money, but we had a good drama department.'

Failing his Eleven Plus meant that Craig couldn't go to a grammar school and he went instead to Hilbre High School in West Kirby. Former pupils also include Olympic cyclist Chris Boardman and members of the English indie rock group The Coral. Here he didn't enjoy the lessons too much, but threw himself into the drama society.

Brenda Davies, a drama teacher at the school, remembers him coming into a casting session for *Oliver!* in 1981: 'My jaw nearly hit the floor when he got up on stage. He had such timing and range and he had stage presence for a 13-year-old. I thought: "What have we here?"' She probably didn't realise that he'd already made his stage debut in the same play at Frodsham Church of England Primary School with his sister Lea. As the then headmaster Peter Mason recalled: 'Both Daniel and his older sister Lea were very good. I could tell even then that Daniel was gifted. I was sorry when they left the school.' Hindsight is a wonderful thing.

He went on to grace many school productions, including *The Real Inspector Hound* which was also staged at the Liverpool Garden Festival. In it, he played an unlovable theatre critic, a breed he was regularly to encounter much later in life.

It seems that he had female admirers even back then, too, as an old school friend, Adam Brierley, tells it: 'He was always popular with the girls. He would always have new girlfriends and keep the relations on an on-and-off basis. As well as being a good laugh, he was also quite a deep person, quite thoughtful and mature

Above: Daniel strikes a menacing pose on stage with the Heswall Woolgatherers.

– and the girls liked that a lot.'

One in particular has very fond memories. Helen Gowland dated Daniel for two years when they were fellow pupils at Hilbre High School. 'He was a lovely lad and I'm sure he has not changed much,' she told *The Daily Mirror*, when it was announced he was to be Bond. 'He still looks much like he did when he was fifteen. We were close and I have good memories of Daniel. I am really pleased he has gone on to make such a success of himself.' She also sadly recalled that she had wanted to pursue an acting career, but her dad was set on her being a secretary.

When Daniel was unveiled as the new James Bond, the tabloids printed a lot of unkind rumours that his nickname was 'Potato Head' at school due to the cragginess of his face. He has hotly denied this and if, as former girlfriend Gowland claims, he looked pretty much as he does now, it would seem unlikely unless the nickname was born out of jealousy.

As well as acting, he also had a brief stint as the lead singer in a band called Inner Voices, run by his aforementioned friend Adam Brierley. As Brierley remembers: 'We needed a front man as my voice was in the middle of breaking. Danny was always in shows and clearly had a good stage presence. He was always a big character, and was quite tall for his age, fifteen at the time. He wasn't fazed by anyone. And he could sing. His style was like Mark Knopfler from Dire Straits. But he left the band when he decided he was better at acting.'

If his brief, and painful, stab at singing in Steven Spielberg's film *Munich* was anything to go by, he definitely made the right choice. On the basis of that performance, he's far more likely to win an Oscar than he is a Grammy.

As well as acting, the young Daniel was a keen sportsman and played rugby for the Birkenhead Park Colts. As his proud dad Tim asserts: 'He can look after himself alright. As a lad he was a tough rugby player and he would probably have become a professional if things hadn't

turned out differently.' This explains how he was able to beef up so effectively for his role in *Casino Royale*. He continues to be a keen rugby fan and goes to games with his dad. As he told an *Observer* journalist in 2006: 'We're off to Dublin next weekend to watch the last game of the Six Nations. It's not the coolest thing in the world to like, but I've been watching it since I was a kid.' As well as the sport, he also enjoys the camaraderie and the drinking that goes with it, explaining: 'Your feet don't touch the ground!'

Daniel's sporting interests weren't entirely confined to rugby, however, as he admits to being a lifelong fan of Liverpool Football Club. Away from the sports pitches, though, his favourite pastime was going to the cinema. His local cinema ran double bills and he used to eat them up, whatever was on: 'I just went and watched movies, from *Quest For Fire* to *Blade Runner*. I thought, "F***, this is what I want to do."'

Having watched lots of screen deaths, he also decided he needed to practice getting shot as it might come in handy later on. The beach at the Wirral proved very useful to this endeavour. He got so good that he mightily impressed the crew on his later film *Layer Cake*: 'We were doing these squib shots and this guy said, "God, you're really good at this." I said, "This is why I became an actor". I used to stand at the top of a sand dune and my mate would stand below and shoot me and I'd throw myself down. Then I'd go, "right, now let's do that with a shotgun."' Squib shots are the small explosions used to make on-screen gunfire look and sound realistic.

This certainly constituted dedication to a career that he was clearly desperate to pursue, as he later admitted: 'I was always going to move to London. I always wanted to be an actor. I had the arrogance to believe I couldn't be anything else.'

But it was unclear to the young Daniel how he might actually achieve his aim. Having failed his 'O' levels and dropped out of a foundation course, his mother worried that her son would flounder in

Liverpool. This was the early eighties when Britain was in the grip of heavy unemployment and she didn't want him to become another statistic. So she sent him along to the Manchester auditions for the National Youth Theatre.

'It was 1984 and in Liverpool, it was just the worst time,' he later told a magazine. 'It was a pit. Everything was depressed as f***. She realised I wasn't going to get my exams and she was worried enough to want me to get out.' Describing himself as 'failing miserably' at school, he jokingly recalled: 'My mum obviously thought, "Why won't this smelly eating machine leave my house?"'

Carol's thoughts were obviously a lot kinder than that, and she was overjoyed when he succeeded in winning a place on the prestigious NYT training scheme. Having made sure he knew how to cook – 'My mother gave me a real kick toward cooking, which was that if I wanted to eat, I'd better know how to do it myself' – she packed him off to London at the age of seventeen to launch himself on what was to be a rocky but thrilling adventure.

While Daniel was never to return to the north full time, he still harbours a nostalgic fondness for the place where he grew up, telling *The Times* in 1999: 'A weight drops off you when you get past Watford. People say "Morning!" And when you go shopping up north, you don't have to spend £50 every time. A newspaper, Sellotape and some drawing pins doesn't cost a fiver.' As he left for London in 1985, he was about to find out just how expensive a place the capital city could be.

2

LONDON AND
DRAMA SCHOOL

When Daniel Craig set off to London from Liverpool in 1985

with no qualifications to his name, he knew he had to do well.

There was no going back and, while his mother had been

incredibly supportive of his acting ambitions, she was also

very worried about her only son's future.

It had been Carol who had packed him off to the Manchester auditions for the National Youth Theatre, she had also laid down some conditions for his early departure to the capital city. As she later told *The Mirror*: 'I said if he wasn't going to university, he must promise to get into a top drama school – or go back to school.'

But first he was headed for the prestigious summer course at the National Youth Theatre in Holloway, north London. Not one of the city's most glamorous locales, it was nonetheless home to an organisation that had given a start to actors as famous as Sir Derek Jacobi, Daniel Day-Lewis, Helen Mirren and Timothy Spall.

Not a drama school as such, the NYT offers courses in all aspects of theatre to young people from the ages of thirteen to twenty-one. Every year, roughly 3,000 applicants apply for 500 places so to win a spot, especially given the list of the NYT's illustrious alumni, is considered a great start to any actor's career.

A short course involving improvisation and tuition finishes with a performance to other members of the NYT that is closed to the public. Those who successfully complete this course then become a member of the NYT acting company and are able to audition for roles in productions.

As Daniel recalls: 'It was good for me. It's like a big youth club but it's also quite serious because they use professional crews and you quickly get involved with what real theatre is like.' He certainly seemed to make a favourable impression as he was cast immediately as the Governor of Cyprus in *Othello* later that year. A spokesman for the NYT confirmed: 'Being cast that quickly is very unusual for new members.'

It must have been a major boost for the seventeen-year-old Daniel, who had only his own dreams and the positive words of his drama teachers to encourage him to believe that a career as a professional actor might be within his grasp. Things

were extremely tough financially as, even though he was cast in at least one NYT production for the next five years, he was earning very little.

As television presenter Jamie Theakston, who appeared alongside Daniel in TS Eliot's *Murder In The Cathedral* and *Marat/Sade* in 1989, recalls: 'I had a fantastic time at the NYT but I found it very hard financially. At one point I was so hard up I was forced to share a really squalid room with three other NYT members. So when most of my contemporaries applied to drama school, I decided that, much as I loved acting, I didn't love it enough to spend the rest of my life having to eke out a living.'

Daniel, however, was made of sterner stuff and continued to pursue his dreams. He supplemented his income between NYT productions with a series of low-paid jobs including bar work and working in restaurant kitchens. He later told American morning TV hosts Regis and Kelly, that he was even offered a job as a waiter on the QE2. His dad, for one, was proud of his tenacity and ability to adapt, telling *The Sunday Mirror*: 'He used to work behind the bar of a pub in Portobello Road, London, and he could certainly handle himself if fights kicked off.'

It wasn't a particularly prosperous or happy time for Daniel, as he later told *The Times*: 'When you first come here you have to survive. You tend to end up being selfish. You have to live off people's floors and rent property and you end up doing runners. I've done awful things to survive, because I've had no money.' Any landlords who were done out of rent in the mid-80s and caught *Casino Royale* on the big screen may well have found their man, and their pay day, some twenty years later.

Daniel is quick to acknowledge that his struggle wasn't that special, just the sort of thing that thousands of aspiring actors have to go through, and he refutes claims that he was particularly ambitious: 'Driven at seventeen? Some seventeen-year-olds may be driven but I certainly wasn't! I was just like everybody else, living day to

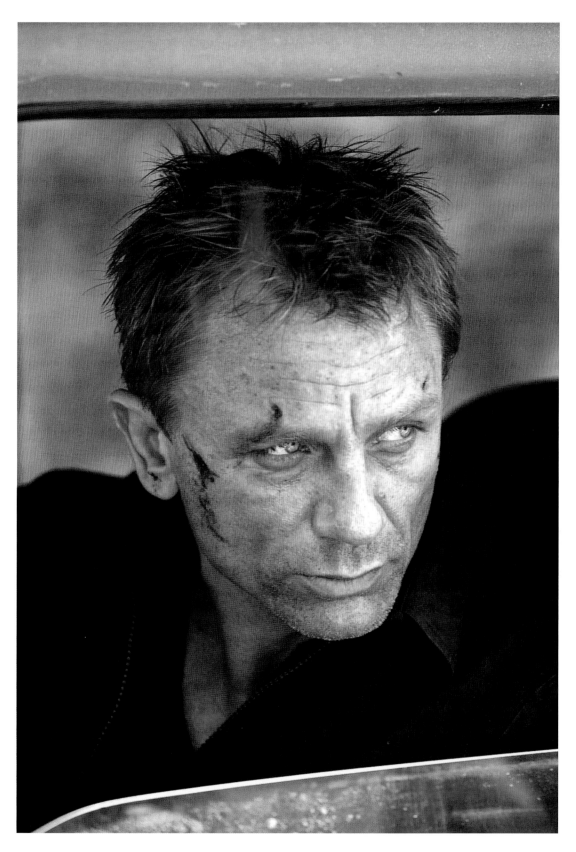

day, getting on with it… I was no Dick
Whittington. At that age bravery doesn't
come into it – you do what you do. You
either come here and fall flat on your face,
or you survive and become successful.'
There were also rumours that he had once
been so broke that he had a spell sleeping
on park benches. In a television interview
with Michael Parkinson, he claimed that
this was exaggeration: 'I slept out a couple
of nights, usually because I was too drunk
to get home.'

While he continued to be cast in NYT
productions, playing Malcolm in *Night
Shriek* in 1986, Tibalt in *Romeo And Juliet*
in 1987 and Simon Schachava in Bertolt
Brecht's *The Caucasian Chalk Circle* in
1988, his applications to drama school
were unsuccessful until three years later
in 1988.

Having applied to several drama
schools, several times without result, he
was finally accepted on the prestigious
three-year BA (Hons) Acting course at
the Guildhall School of Music and Drama
in 1988 at the age of twenty. Now based
at the world-famous Barbican Centre
in London, the Guildhall is a highly-
regarded drama school which has been
training actors since 1880. To win a place
here was a big deal and it meant that he'd
finally fulfilled the deal he'd done with his
mother. There was no threat of having to
go back to school now.

Daniel was certainly blessed with some
talented contemporaries at the Guildhall.
Among those with whom he trained were
Rhys Ifans, who went on to become his
co-star in *Enduring Love*, Damian Lewis,
Alastair McGowan, Ewan McGregor

Above: Daniel with his friend and fellow graduate from the Guildhall School of Music and Drama, Rhys Ifans.

(whom he allegedly beat to the Bond role), Joseph Fiennes and Fay Ripley.

Despite the fact that he'd finally realised his goal of making it to drama school, he doesn't appear to have particularly fond memories of this period. When asked about his time at the Guildhall he later said in an interview: 'I'm not sure what I got out of it, apart from the discipline of getting up in the morning and knowing not to shout when you're backstage.'

He also told *The Times* in 1999: 'For three years you talk shit to each other. If it works, it keeps the sparks going, and you hit the industry with lovely open eyes, not cynical.' The Guildhall doesn't seem to have taken it personally, though, having invited their famous old boy to speak to current students several times. 'I suppose my advice would be to stick with it and make something happen. I was lucky to do a bit of TV that paid the rent and a bit of theatre, which pays f*** all.'

It might not have paid well, but he enjoyed his productions with they NYT and the opportunities for travel that they afforded. In 1989 his role as the fourth knight in *Murder In The Cathedral*

took him to Moscow along with Jamie Theakston when the NYT presented the first ever production of the play in the city in the Moscow Art Theatre. The following year saw him take the important role of married lover Leonardo in Federico Garcia Lorca's *Blood Wedding*, a play that toured to Valencia in Spain.

He recalls the travelling with great affection: 'I'd come back from a job and be in the car coming from the airport and I'd go to the driver, "Take me somewhere else." I loved being nomadic.'

When later asked by an upmarket women's magazine what he was like at twenty-one, he was very definite in his reply: 'Indestructible. At least I thought I was. Between the ages of eighteen and twenty-one you do feel invincible. It's a landmark, the point at which you become a man.'

One woman who testified to his manhood at this time in a later 'kiss and tell' was Marina Pepper. Now a Lib Dem councillor living in East Sussex, she told of an alleged six-month fling with Daniel when he was eighteen and she was twenty. They apparently met at a bar in Notting Hill and, as kiss and tells go, this was a positive tale as she enthused about his sexual stamina and sensitivity. Despite the rave review, Daniel was no doubt uncomfortable with the story, consistently having tried to keep his private life private.

Although he may have had some reservations about his time at Guildhall, by this time Daniel had discovered a joy in acting that was to remain with him and serve as a vital support in the tough years that were still ahead. In his conversation with friend and artist Sam Taylor-Wood in *Interview* magazine, he compared acting to drugs. 'You're also opening yourself up and saying, "I'm going to allow people to judge what I do". That's a big step. The most important thing to remember is that once you've done it, there's no going back. And whether you make it or not, whether you make money or not, it's a career. And actually, there's nothing like it. Because once you've gotten some real fulfilment

from something, once you can say, "I've moved someone; I've made someone think differently", it becomes like a drug, and you want to keep doing it.'

So, the bug that he'd caught at the Everyman Theatre in Liverpool had definitely developed into a permanent infection. Despite many knock backs, he had shown enough self-belief to keep on applying to drama schools until he was finally accepted. Neither was he above taking on any job that was on offer in order to make ends meet until he realised his dream. There were indignities that would later resurface once he became the world's most super-cool spy. One journalist, keen to mock the new Bond, highlighted a voice-over Daniel had done for Beer Paradise, which the journo had found circulating on the Internet – 'Open every day on the South Access Road, near the Crown Point retail park, Liverpool'. Daniel freely admits that it was playing Mr Marmite, in a Marmite jumper, at a shopping centre in Reading, that finally won him his Equity card. It's hardly fair to criticise a Bond actor for what he did at the very outset of his career. Sean Connery, after all, was a bodybuilder and artists' model, while Roger Moore appeared wearing cardigans in knitting patterns. The important thing is, as Daniel was discovering, that you should never give up. It wasn't all to be plain sailing for him, even with the Guildhall on his CV. He may have felt that posh boys had the advantage in Thatcher's Britain, but he wasn't about to let that stop him taking to the screen, small or large.

Previous spread: Pictured here at Sydney Harbour Bridge, becoming 'James Bond' certainly suited Daniel's love of travel.
Opposite: TV presenter and actor Jamie Theakston was a fellow National Youth Theatre student with Daniel in the 1980s.

3

FINDING THE BIG BREAK

When he left drama school, with three years of training and a

wealth of contacts under his belt, Daniel was under no illusions

that an easy life awaited him. The menial work in bars and kitchens

would continue as he chipped away at making it in the often

confusing world of professional acting.

As a working class boy, he felt himself at a disadvantage in the dramatic climate of the early nineties. Upper class dramas exemplified by classic TV productions such as *Brideshead Revisited* and the films of Ismail Merchant and James Ivory were very much the vogue – *Howards End* and *The Remains Of The Day* would both come out over the next two years.

Daniel worked hard to lose his accent and fit in, explaining that the 'classless' accent at that time was still relatively posh. When asked years later in *The Observer* about losing his regional accent, he said: 'Exactly! Exachtly! What has happened to it? It's gone! Believe me, I know. I even grew my fringe long. Well, you know, when I left drama school it was Merchant Ivory or nothing!' He was never cast as the posh boy, though, and he later explained, with more than a touch of chippiness: 'Nah, I think they figured out that I was common as muck.'

It wasn't his impeccable working class credentials that casting directors seemed to recognise in this early part of his career though, rather a menace that would serve him so well later on. The combination of blond hair, piercing blue eyes and simmering broodiness saw him cast as a long line of baddies in an eclectic range of productions.

His first stroke of luck came before he left Guildhall when he was cast in a big-budget Hollywood movie *Power Of One*. With Stephen Dorff in the starring role and Morgan Freeman and John Gielgud in the supporting cast, the movie's cast had excellent credentials. Based on a novel by Bryce Courtenay, it was an anti-apartheid drama about a boy who beats bullies through the magic of boxing.

Adopting a very convincing and harsh Afrikaans accent, Daniel was cast as the brutal Sergeant Botha. A former school bully turned violent and corrupt cop, he was the arch villain pitted against Dorff's hero. Sporting a Nazi tattoo and a horrifically racist attitude, Botha battered and murdered his way through the movie before getting his fatal comeuppance. The film was directed by John G Avildsen, who was also responsible for the original *Rocky* boxing movie with Sylvester Stallone, as well as all three instalments of *The Karate Kid*. While it didn't receive a brilliant critical reception, it nonetheless showed that Daniel could hold his own on a film set alongside major stars of the time.

Shot mainly in Zimbabwe and at the posh Charterhouse School in Godalming, Surrey, it seems that the movie left Daniel feeling fairly overawed by the whole experience. He later told *The Times*: 'After leaving drama school I was terrified. It made no sense to me whatsoever. On set, people would call my name and I'd be like "Yes?!" I wish I had someone to say to me "Relax, everything's fine. It's not the end of the world."'

Although acquitting himself well, despite the understandable nerves of a novice, this wasn't a role that was immediately to lead to greater things. This

Previous spread: Daniel as 'Lieutenant Berry' in *Sharpe's Eagle.*
Right: Stephen Dorff, star of the 1992 movie *Power of One* in which Daniel won his first film role.
Opposite: Daniel appeared in the very last episode of the ITV Drama, *Boon.*

must have been hard to deal with at the time but, in retrospect, he was glad that his career didn't take off on the back of a nasty Nazi villain: 'It didn't happen for me then, and it was pretty good that it didn't. I'm so glad I'm not playing nasty South African policemen.' There were plenty more baddies in his future, though, as he headed back to England and threw himself into the endless round of auditions. In the absence of more movie roles, television was the obvious stepping stone for an actor determined to earn a living and gain much needed experience.

His first foray into television was a 'blink-and-you'd-miss-it' walk-on in *Anglo Saxon Attitudes*, a three-part ITV adaptation of the Angus Wilson novel of the same name. It also featured a sixteen-year-old Kate Winslet, with whom Daniel would work again in a Disney film in 1995. Adapted by the famous Andrew Davies, it would go on to win a BAFTA for best serial, though this would not greatly benefit Daniel.

Next up was another tiny part in the very last episode of popular ITV drama *Boon*. Set in Birmingham with the late Michael Elphick starring as a fireman turned private eye, this popular drama was running out of steam by the seventh and final series. No doubt Daniel found the pay packet and the experience more than welcome, though. And finally in television terms for 1992 came *Covington Cross*. This peculiar medieval drama starred Nigel Terry as widower Sir Thomas Grey and Cherie Lunghi as his love interest, Lady Elizabeth. Daniel appeared simply as 'walkway guard' in the pilot episode, the only one to be shown in the UK.

He was given much more of a chance to shine in 1992 in the theatre production *No Remission* by Rod Williams. This prison drama was staged at the Lyric Theatre, Hammersmith by the Midnight Theatre Company. Daniel played an ex-paratrooper convicted of murder who goes mad when his cellmates reveal that the woman he's in love with is a common slut. His performance moved a critic from *The*

Independent to note that he: 'contains his violence like an unexploded mine.' Being mentioned in a national newspaper review at this stage of his career must have given Daniel's confidence a major boost.

Another hugely significant event of 1992 was Daniel's marriage to his Scottish actress girlfriend Fiona Loudon. She was already five months pregnant with his daughter when the pair married in Edinburgh. The marriage would end in divorce two years later but they have maintained a civilised relationship to this day and he is very close to his daughter, Ella. Extremely protective of her privacy, he won't mention her by name in interviews. She lives in London with her mother and he has said that fatherhood is one of the most amazing things in his life.

After his brief and low-profile forays into television in 1992, the following year saw Daniel become a little more visible. *Between The Lines* was a BBC1 police series that was both a critical and ratings success. Starring Neil Pearson, Siobhan Redmond and Tom Georgeson as cops investigating corruption within the force, it ran for three series from 1992 to 1994. Each episode had a self-contained story with longer-running storylines throughout the series. Daniel guest-starred in one episode as Joe Nance, a Neo-Nazi sympathiser with brutal tendencies. More than a few echoes, then, of his role as Sergeant Botha in *Power Of One*. His character, however, turned out to be an undercover cop whom the investigation squad thought had 'gone native', or become too involved in the brutal, racist world he was infiltrating.

With another more than competent brute on his show-reel, he found himself working with blue-eyed boy Neil Pearson again in an episode of hit comedy *Drop The Dead Donkey*. Set in a TV newsroom, this satirical sitcom was a big Friday night hit for Channel 4 and also starred Stephen Tompkinson and Jeff Rawle. Daniel appeared as Fixx, an unsavoury squatter and ringleader of a group of thieves that also included station manager

Opposite: A sultry publicity shot taken in the mid-90s as Daniel was beginning to make a name for himself.

Right: Sean Patrick Flannery in *The Young Indiana Jones Chronicles*.
Opposite: As the brutish 'Lieutenant Berry' in *Sharpe's Eagle*, Daniel played Sharpe's enemy, attempting to shoot him in the back before himself being killed.

George's (Rawle) wayward daughter. Another baddie, his comeuppance came with the humiliation of being forced to stand on one leg and sing *The Birdie Song*. If you manage to catch this performance repeated on the digital channels, you'll see again that music's loss was definitely acting's gain.

Daniel also added his name to the credits of one of British television's most long-standing drama series in 1993, *Heartbeat*, a soft-centred, nostalgic police drama set in a never-ending 1960s in rural Yorkshire. Still enormously popular with viewers, the show is now in its eighteenth series. Its guest stars have included faces as diverse as Charlotte Church, David Essex, Lulu, Ralf Little of *The Royle Family* and impressionist Jon Culshaw. Daniel appeared in an episode of the second series when former *EastEnder* Nick Berry played the central character of PC Nick Rowan. He was cast as another ne'er do well, Peter Begg, a grandson who returns to Aidensfield much to the horror of his ex-girlfriend.

While the elderly, blue-rinse brigade may have lapped up his 'bad boy'

when they tuned in to that particular *Heartbeat* storyline, Daniel reached a younger, more upmarket demographic with his appearance in *Sharpe's Eagle*. A swashbuckling adventure starring Sean Bean that still returns to our screens for the occasional special, *Sharpe* is set in the Napoleonic Wars. Based on the novels by Bernard Cornwell, it features Bean as the titular character taking on all manner of despicable foes.

Step forward Daniel Craig as the number one foe in *Sharpe's Eagle*, the second instalment of the drama. He played Lieutenant Berry, a brutish snob who despises Sharpe for his low birth and is assigned by one of his superiors to dispose of him. After abusing a woman Sharpe is protecting, he then attempts to shoot him in the back but is himself killed by Sharpe's sergeant, Harper.

Daniel's run of villainous roles continued that year with a part in the American made-for-TV drama *The Adventures Of Young Indiana Jones,* also known as *The Young Indiana Jones Chronicles*. Designed as a prequel to the blockbusting *Indiana Jones* movies,

it starred Sean Patrick Flanery as the youthful Jones and was created and executive produced by the mighty George Lucas. Daniel featured in an episode entitled *Palestine, 1917* in which the young Indy helps British and Australian troops take the city of Beersheba, then occupied by the Turks.

Daniel is again cast as a villain, this time the head of German intelligence in Beersheba, Captain Schiller. He'd spent so much of his professional life in uniform by this point he must have thought he'd signed up for national service. The episode was also notable for the inclusion of a young Catherine Zeta Jones, veiled and alluring as a belly dancer spy named Maya.

Again it was theatre that was to win him the most attention that year with a high profile production at the National Theatre of *Angels In America: A Gay Fantasia On National Themes* by Tony Kushner. In the second part of the epic, *Perestroika*, he played Joe Pitt, a secretly gay Republican Mormon. The play was a huge hit and

gained Daniel a lot of positive reviews and attention. The play was described in *TheDaily Mail* as an 'altogether dynamic tour de force' and ran to three hours and forty minutes.

The following year saw Daniel appear in another theatrical production, *The Rover*, by Aphra Behn. Staged by the Women's Playhouse Trust, this restoration comedy ran in the Jacob Street Film Studios where ITV filmed fire-fighting drama *London's Burning*. At 14,000 square feet, it was a massive space. The director and set designer Jules Wright covered the floor in red earth, the actors using rickshaws to negotiate the massive set.

The story tells of a raucous night out of three men in Naples. Daniel played Blunt, an English country gentlemen who is convinced that a girl has fallen in love with him only to be humiliated when she turns out to be a prostitute. It was a plot echoing that of his 1992 production *No Remission*. His co-stars were Dougray Scott, who went on to star in cult American TV

drama *Desperate Housewives*, and Andy Serkis, who became the voice of Gollum in *The Lord Of The Rings*.

Daniel's one foray into television in 1994 was in a peculiar Screen Two film for BBC2. A black comedy based on a novel by Romain Gary, *Genghis Cohn* starred Robert Lindsay as Otto Schatz, a former SS officer who is haunted by the ghost of a Jewish comedian he had murdered during the war. The ghost, played by Anthony Sher, insists that his murderer should convert to Judaism. Daniel played Lieutenant Guth, the policeman who replaces Schatz when he has a breakdown. While the off-the-wall comedy was generally well-received, Daniel's role wasn't significant enough for him to be singled out for particular praise.

Another project he worked on in 1994 but which wasn't released until 1996 was *Saint-Ex*. A drama documentary directed by Anand Tucker, it told the story of Antoine de Saint-Exupery, a famous aviator and author of the children's book *The Little Prince*. A highbrow, moody film which interspersed documentary interviews with drama, it received its premiere at the London Film Festival in November 1996 and was shown on British television that Christmas. Daniel played Guillaumet, the lead character's best friend and fellow aviator. It was a foretaste of the heavyweight, yet interesting, projects Daniel would lean toward later in his career when he was in a better position to choose projects rather than take what he could get.

His only screen work to be released in 1995 most definitely fell into the latter 'take what he could get' category. *A Kid In King Arthur's Court* was a Disney movie directed by Michael Gottlieb and shot in the UK and Hungary. Loosely based on Mark Twain's story *A Connecticut Yankee In King Arthur's Court*, it told the tale of a modern American teen who turns up at the Round Table.

Thomas Ian Nicholas, who later went on to star in the hit comedy movie *American Pie*, played the displaced teenager Calvin Russell, bringing rock and roll and skating to Anglo Saxon Britain.

Daniel played Master Kane, a commoner who is charged with teaching Calvin the art of combat. He also happens to be in love with Princess Sarah who is played by a young Kate Winslet. Their paths had crossed briefly before in *Anglo Saxon Attitudes*. The film went straight to video in the UK and, given the eccentricity of the plot, it was probably just as well. When Daniel told *Elle* magazine in 2006: 'Well, there will always be some films on the video shelves I'm not too proud of, put it that way,' it wouldn't be stretching the imagination too much to believe that this might be one of them.

What Daniel had achieved in the five years since he left drama school was to accumulate a great deal of varied and valuable experience. As well as small parts in Hollywood movies and roles in epic London theatrical productions, he had also increased his screen time on television. His CV may have been disparate but he had worked with some great actors and directors and built up even more contacts and confidence for the future.

The following year, 1996, was to see him get his big break with a meaty role in a television drama that would have everyone talking. As Geordie Peacock in *Our Friends In The North*, he impressed himself on the British public and became a name rather than just a face that perhaps looked vaguely familiar.

4

FRIENDS LIKE THESE

Anyone watching Daniel Craig's career with keen interest in 1995

could have been forgiven for thinking that it was floundering

slightly. All that could be seen in that year was the Disney movie

that went straight-to-video in the UK, *A Kid In King Arthur's Court*.

In reality, Daniel spent much of 1995 working on his most exciting project to date; one that was going to catapult him to mainstream recognition when it was first aired in January 1996.

Our Friends In The North was a sprawling, well-made television saga about a group of friends from Newcastle. Written and developed by Peter Flannery from a play that he had staged with the Royal Shakespeare Company, it followed the lives of four friends from 1964 to 1995.

Both an instant critical hit and one of those shows that people talked about after each episode was aired, *Our Friends* was destined to become a British television classic. Named No 25 in a list of 100 Greatest British Television Programmes in a British Film Institute Poll in 2000, it was also showered with BAFTAs and RTS awards.

When he started filming on the nine-part series in late 1994, Daniel can't have known how great an impact his latest television serial would have. Having read the scripts, he was quietly confident about the quality of the project, but didn't want to tempt fate. As he told *The Times* in 2004: 'Mark Strong and I secretly would get drunk and say, "this could be quite good". But we were very nervous about saying it. When you are starting out, usually it's about ninety per cent disappointment, so you tend to harden yourself. It's a bullshit approach, but it makes it easier to deal with the rejection you get three times a week if you go for interviews.'

Daniel was cast as George 'Geordie' Peacock, one of four friends and the one who would go on the biggest journey of all throughout the 31-year span of the drama. A wannabe popstar at the beginning, he was forced to confront his violent, alcoholic father and give up his dreams. He hitchhiked down to London where he eventually fell in with a crook and pimp called Benny Barrett. The latter was played by respected actor Malcolm McDowell, who had been lured over from America to make what

was a rare television appearance. A decent man at heart, Geordie is led astray by a combination of naiveté and weakness. Sucked into a world of vice and corruption, he has an affair and falls in love with a prostitute who happens to be his boss's mistress. In revenge, Benny sets him up with the police and he is jailed for three years. There's not much for Geordie when he gets out and he ends up as a homeless drifter who is eventually jailed again after setting fire to his mattress in a hostel. By the end of the drama, he has escaped from prison and is reunited with his three friends in Newcastle. The drama ends with him walking across the iconic Tyne Bridge to the soundtrack of Oasis' *Don't Look Back In Anger*.

This was a huge role for a young actor and Daniel made the most of it. Always utterly believable as a man for whom hope eventually dies, his struggles through life were movingly portrayed. While much of his story is grim, it was impossible to tear your eyes away from his emotional performance. *Radio Times* film editor Andrew Collins pointed out over a decade later: '*Our Friends In The North* was the making of Daniel Craig. Geordie Peacock had the most extreme ride of all the drama's characters, decamping to London to work for gangster Malcolm McDowell, losing everything and going to prison. His transformation from young hipster to haggard, haunted vagrant in middle age was spotless.'

Meaty, well-structured scripts and great co-stars also helped. The aforementioned Mark Strong played Terry 'Tosker' Cox whose singing ambitions were eventually dropped in favour of a fruit and vegetable business. He married Mary Soulsby, a frustrated intellectual played by Gina McKee who had been in love with Dominic 'Nicky' Hutchinson. An idealistic young man with politics on his mind, Nicky was played by Christopher Ecclestone who had already made his mark in *Cracker* and went on to play *Doctor Who* when that series was reinvented in the early noughties.

Previous Spread: Daniel with long, flowing locks and Alex Kingston in the 1996 ITV series *Moll Flanders.*

At a time when digital and satellite TV had yet to completely fragment viewing, *Our Friends* had a big impact on the nation. Jeffrey Richards in *The Independent* put it into context: 'The serial captivated much of the country, sketching a panoramic view of life in Britain from the Sixties to the Nineties… At once sweeping and intimate, both moving and angry, simultaneously historical and contemporary, it has followed in the distinguished footsteps of BBC series such as *Boys From The Blackstuff*.'

After the odd dodgy Disney movie and frustratingly small parts in television, *Our Friends* was just the psychological fillip and career boost that Daniel needed. As he recalled in 2006: 'It helped me start to enjoy myself again. It was a great chance to work with that great group of actors. I showed it to a friend the other day and it stood up. Gina (McKee) and Mark (Strong) and Chris (Ecclestone) were fantastic. They all seem fabulously real. It was because we spent time discovering things about each other. It was like being taught all over again how to make a character and get it watchable. Like a year with a Russian theatre.'

A leading role in such a high profile series certainly meant that it was a lot easier for Daniel to be seen by casting

directors. 'It was simple really,' he said in an interview in 1999. 'I couldn't get a lead in a television series because I didn't have a track record. But as soon as I did that, I was offered them. It was a kick in the rear end up the stairs.'

Another role in a popular television show later that year kept him in the public eye. He played Jemmy Seagrave in a rollicking adaptation of Daniel Defoe's *Moll Flanders* starring Alex Kingston. A four-part drama on ITV, it was notable for its bawdy sex scenes, many of which featured Daniel. Jemmy was a love interest for Moll, a fellow fortune-hunter posing as an aristocrat who proves more than a match for her. After much to-ing and fro-ing, the pair end up together, albeit being transported to America for their respective sins. Much talked about, not least because

of its raunchiness, it did more for Alex Kingston's profile than for Daniel's as she went on to star in the hit American TV series *E.R.*

His other television outings that year were in an American-made drama *Tales From The Crypt* and a British crime drama *Kiss And Tell*. Inspired by the horror comics of William M Gaines, *Tales From The Crypt* was made into seven TV series by leading American drama network HBO (Home Box Office). Daniel featured in an episode of the final series as an ex-con involved in murderous dodgy dealings at an advertising agency. American viewers who watched *Tales From The Crypt* at the time would be hard pressed to reconcile Daniel's shifty character with the suave James Bond they now know and love.

Opposite: Daniel as 'James "Jemmy" Seagrave', a supposed aristocratic gentleman. Above: 'Jemmy' and 'Moll' both turn out to be total rogues and are sentenced to be transported to America.

Right: Daniel as 'Detective Matt Kearney' in *Kiss and Tell*.

Cast as a tortured cop trying to prove that a husband had murdered his missing wife, Daniel popped up in *Kiss And Tell*, a not particularly memorable ITV crime drama. He played Detective Matt Kearney who talks his ex-girlfriend, who happens to be a psychologist, into trying to extract a confession from the husband by becoming romantically involved with him. Designed to capitalise on similar stories that were in the news at the time, this had all the hallmarks of a rush job and neither its plot nor its characterisation were either particularly well conceived or sufficiently gripping.

Viewers would next see Daniel playing another policeman in the following year's *The Ice House*. An adaptation of one of Minette Walter's best-selling crime novels, this was his first leading role in a television drama. He played DS Andy McLoughlin, an alcoholic Scottish cop, and the role gave him plenty of opportunities to showcase his brooding intensity to maximum effect. The cast included veteran actor Corin Redgrave and Royal Shakespeare

Company favourite Frances Barber.

The plot involved three women living in a big country house whose lives were thrown into chaos when a body is found in an outlying 'ice house'. McLoughlin's personal life is in tatters as his wife has left him for another man and he ends up jeopardising the case by becoming involved with one of the suspects, Anne Cattrell (Kitty Aldridge). As Adam Sweeting in *The Guardian* put it, in a delicious premonition of what was to come: 'Emotionally battered, nursing a drink problem, happy to become sexually involved with suspects and nonchalantly ignoring the law whenever he feels like it, McLoughlin would make James Bond feel like a desk-bound dullard counting the days to his pension.'

The beleaguered Detective Sergeant has rediscovered his humanity by the end of the drama and all ends reasonably well for his character. While the plot was written off by many critics, the acting came in for particular praise and Craig was described in *The Independent* as having 'an almost feral degree of erotic appeal'. His other TV outing in 1997 was in a schlock horror series called *The Hunger*, introduced by Terence Stamp. He was in an episode called *Menage A Trois* which co-starred older American actress Karen Black and Lena Headey (now saving the world in *Terminator: The Sarah Connor Chronicles*). Daniel handled several sex scenes with the glamorous Headey rather well but there is little else to commend this rather bizarre tale.

Another work that surfaced in 1997 was *Obsession*, a German TV movie which is mostly notable for being where Daniel met his long-term girlfriend Heike Makatsch. In *Obsession* he plays John MacHale, a Zimbabwean wood-cutter working in Berlin. Obsessed with the tightrope walkers who negotiated Niagara, he also gets involved in a love triangle between a girl band member (Makatsch) and a French scientist. If it sounds confusing, then it is and only Daniel Craig completists will want to bother digging it out on DVD.

Daniel's theatre work that year was far better received. He starred alongside Rupert Graves as Mickey, a divorced Hollywood casting agent in David Rabe's 1984 play *Hurlyburly*. Staged by Sir Peter Hall's company at the Old Vic in London, it was described by *The Times* as 'worth attention if it had been relegated to the bottom of a plague pit in Mortlake'. Featuring sex, drugs and debauchery, it was a demonstration of the horrible things Hollywood can do to man's soul. The play's opening night was disrupted by a bomb scare and the actors reassembled in a square opposite the theatre and finished the play outdoors, much to the delight of the press.

At the end of 1997, Daniel began shooting on *Love And Rage*. Directed by Cathal Black, this was a film loosely based on a real life story from the end of the 19th century. Shot on Achill Island off the coast of County Mayo in the west of Ireland, it told of an ill-fated and sadistic love affair between English landowner Agnes McDonnell (Greta Scacchi) and local man James Lynchehaun (Daniel Craig). Lynchehaun was a controversial figure who inspired JM Synge's famous *The Playboy Of The Western World* and Daniel portrayed him as the wild, animal-like manipulator he was supposed to be. With many scenes of sex and violence, this was a disturbing film that was never released theatrically in the UK but received its world premiere at the Irish Film Festival in 1999.

His presence in a far more commercial property released in 1998, albeit in a small role, did much more for Daniel's profile. *Elizabeth*, directed by Shekhar Kapur, starred Cate Blanchett as the young Elizabeth I. Daniel's co-star in *Our Friends*, Christopher Ecclestone, took a starring part as the Duke of Norfolk, virtually stealing the film from Blanchett and Geoffrey Rush, who played the queen's advisor, Sir Francis Walsingham.

Daniel first appears one hour into the film as John Ballard. We first see him kissing the hand of the Pope, played by Sir John Gielgud in his last movie appearance. He is assigned to bring letters to England and charged with assassinating the young Protestant queen. Wading out of the sea in dark robes, he meets up with Ecclestone's Norfolk before swiftly dispatching his aide Thomas Elliot by bashing him over the head with a rock. Having failed in his attempt to bump off the Queen, he is then systematically tortured until he is a bloody mess. This latter was presumably good practice for the torture scene that lay ahead in *Casino Royale*.

He was to find himself tied up again, this time for erotic purposes, in his other film of that year, *Love Is The Devil*. A biographical story about Irish painter Francis Bacon, it detailed the relationship between Bacon and young burglar George Dyer. Daniel played Dyer, the thief who broke into Bacon's studio with the intention of robbing him and ended up staying on and having a relationship with his intended victim. Depicting this involved Daniel spending a lot of screen time in his Y-fronts, often covered in weird substances for the S&M-style sex scenes.

The film was directed by John Maybury, a respected music video director making his first foray into cinema. Daniel and Maybury struck up a lasting friendship, and he went on to be cast in Maybury's 2005 film *The Jacket* alongside Adrien Brody and Keira Knightley. The film, and Daniel's performance, received some very positive reviews and as he recalled in 2007: 'It was the first film that "made me".

Opposite: Daniel with long-term girlfriend Heike Makatsch.

I always wanted to make movies. When I met John Maybury, I knew he was the sort of person I wanted to be involved with because he was genuinely crazy and wonderful.'

Maybury was equally positive about his new, young star: 'He's a real man's man. He has genuine machismo, but he's not afraid to express his sensitive, vulnerable side. He does wounded very well.' The new friends sat down together to pore over their reviews, too. As Daniel recalls: 'We had one in *The Guardian* – they just loved the movie – and another in the *Evening Standard* where it was rubbished, and we both went, "that's success". It's horrible getting bad reviews, but there is a certain amount of truth in every one of them.'

Below: Daniel as 'George Dyer' in *Love is the Devil.*
Opposite: Daniel sported a fluffy, white-blond hairstyle for a *Love is the Devil* photocall in Cannes.

Even mixed reviews meant a certain level of recognition, something every actor on the way up both craves and needs. Daniel's next film, *The Trench*, written and directed by William Boyd, was also to excite the critics. Set during the Battle of the Somme in the First World War, it was described in glowing terms in *The Independent* thus: 'What Boyd and his team have done, given their means, is remarkable… it addresses with profound seriousness and humanity an experience of war that still holds and horrifies, even as it fades from the edges of living memory.' Daniel played platoon Sergeant Telford Winter, a man charged with maintaining discipline within his young troops. He had also to take their minds off the possibility of imminent death.

His performance was both moving and convincing. As he explained at the time: 'I based him on the surrogate father figures you have in your youth. The teacher who was like, "Come on boys, we can do it!" They were children and Winter had to treat them like children. It wasn't just about discipline, it was about stroking and saying "it's going to be OK". A balance between nice and hard.'

Writer/director Boyd, who also became a good friend of Daniel's observed of his performance that he has 'an amazing ability to express emotion of the most poignant kind as well as the most vehement kind. Not all leading men have that – they can do the tough stuff, but they can't always do both.'

His only television outing in 1999 was in a one-hour film for Channel 4. Part of the *Shockers* season of horror/thrillers it was subtitled *The Visitor*. Daniel played the visitor of the title, a man who turns up at the door and moves into a house share, all along pretending to be the long-lost cousin of one of the housemates. As he gradually reveals his sinister side, it's safe to say that all does not end well.

Daniel had three films released in the following year, 2000, and a very mixed bunch they were too. First up was another Hollywood movie, *I Dreamed Of Africa*,

Above: Derek Jacobi played Irish painter 'Francis Bacon' in *Love is the Devil* with Daniel as his lover.

Opposite: Daniel played 'Sergeant Telford Winter' in William Boyd's First World War drama *The Trench*.

based on the autobiography of wealthy Italian woman Kuki Gallmann. She transformed her life after having almost died in a car crash, marrying a man and taking her young son to live on a ranch in Kenya. Kim Basinger, whose career had recently been revitalised by the smash hit *L.A Confidential*, starred as Kuki, a woman who faced deadly wildlife as well as murderous poachers.

Daniel played Declan Fielding, Kuki's good looking, rugged ranch manager but the part offered very little scope and his screen time was limited. The movie was shot over three months in South Africa and did very little at the box office. Basinger, in fact, was nominated for a

Razzie Award (also known as The Golden Raspberries – handed out to the worst performances around the same time as the Oscars) for Worst Actress.

Next came the radically different *Some Voices*. Based on a play by Joe Penhall, this was about a young man suffering from mental illness and was directed by Simon Cellan Jones, who had worked on *Our Friends*. Daniel plays Ray, who suffers a breakdown. His girlfriend is played by Kelly McDonald who had been Ewan McGregor's love interest in *Trainspotting* and his brother is played by David Morrissey, familiar to cinema goers for *Hilary and Jackie*. Daniel compared Ray to Geordie in *Our Friends*. He told *The Times*:

Above: The role of a
young man suffering
from mental illness
proved a challenge for
Daniel in *Some Voices*.

'They're both sympathetic and people who
have no real influence on the world. It
just happens around them and that's their
tragedy. But what the film's really about
is love. Ray's love for his girlfriend and
the love between the brothers. His mental
state cripples that love.'

A psychotherapist was on hand during
filming to advise Daniel on his portrayal
of such a sensitive subject. 'That was
useful,' he later said, 'I don't have anybody
close who's suffered like that but I've got
friends of friends whose wheels have fallen
off, shall we say. What surprises me is
that when they're more stable, they talk

about it and I realise, yes, I feel like that
sometimes. That was where I connected
with Ray.'

There was a scene that required him
to run naked down the Goldhawk Road
in London, a daunting prospect for any
actor. As he explained, though, it was
partially his own fault: 'That was all down
to my good friend Simon who was the
director. The scene was originally written
as me running up and down Goldhawk
Road stripped to the waist and covered
in tomato juice. But then I got drunk one
night in Simon's front room and said, "I
know, I'll do it naked!" The key lesson to

remember there is: don't get drunk with directors.' Having got drunk and proposed the nudity, he also had to have a dram or two to carry it off. 'I drank three large brandies that didn't even touch the sides. We couldn't close the traffic off, but the police were there, so the assistant director went up and said: "Our guy's going to go naked now." The policeman said: "I cannot condone that, but I'll go and get a cup of tea shall I?" They could have arrested me for public exposure.'

A criminal record might have slowed down Daniel's burgeoning international career so it's just as well for that benign policeman. It's hard to imagine James Bond having a conviction for flashing.

His final film of 2000 was the pleasingly bonkers *Hotel Splendide*. Set in a crumbling health spa on a remote isle, it stars Daniel and *Drop The Dead Donkey*'s

Stephen Tompkinson as brothers Ronald and Dezmond, presiding over the ageing health farm. A breath of fresh air comes in the form of Toni Collette as Kath. Ronald's ex-girlfriend, she returns to the island with some fresh food ideas and tries to transform the terrible hotel where colonic irrigation and boiled eel is the norm.

Daniel commented at the time: 'It was so off-the-wall, the sort of Gothic film-making the French do. I think the British are good at being barking mad. There's a part of our character that's not so much eccentric as plain nuts.' Gaining very mixed reviews, it was praised in *The Independent* as a 'laudable British slice of eccentricity.'

From the mid-nineties to the new millennium, Daniel combined some high-profile television with strange art house movies, the odd dodgy film

Above: The co-operation of a friendly policeman helped Daniel to avoid being arrested for indecent exposure during the filming of *Some Voices*.

Right: Kelly McDonald played Daniel's girlfriend in *Some Voices*.
Opposite: Daniel picks up the award for 'Best Actor in an Independent Film' for his performance in *Some Voices* at the British Indepedent Film Awards in October 2000.

that offered decent money and another well-chosen play. Considering how well his performance as Geordie had been received in *Our Friends*, his career still seemed a little slow to take off. This may have been partly because he resisted the sex symbol stereotyping that the press were keen to thrust upon him after that role and the roistering Jemmy Seagrave in *Moll Flanders*. It was reported that

he was getting 500 letters a week from admiring female viewers after *Our Friends* went out. When asked about this by *The Times* in 1999, he got very worked up. 'Rubbish! Rubbish! It didn't happen. OK, I did this thing about eligible bachelors for a women's magazine, thinking it was just part of the press for *Our Friends* but it turned out to be one of those things where you're getting into self promotion…

Above: Daniel played one of the owners of an ageing health farm in *Hotel Splendide*.

And I got loads and loads of letters, which freaked me out completely. I wanted to write back to everyone and say, "I didn't mean it! I'm not eligible. At all!" I think you've got to be kind of sick to want knickers through the post.'

His resistance to being saddled with the sex symbol tag was fierce, and he gave up doing interviews with the lifestyle press for a while. This may have been an admirable move for an actor concerned about being taken seriously but, in the short term, it served to slow the development of his career. Years later, Daniel would intimate that he had already decided his future lay in movies and not in becoming a major British TV star along with the likes of Robson Green and Kevin Whately. 'I thought, "I could earn tons of money doing television, I'll have a house in Portugal, I'll be an alcoholic and I'll be fat, and in ten years, it'll all be over." That's when I thought, "I don't want to do that! I want to make movies."'

Right: Daniel bravely resisted being labelled as a sex symbol, although scenes like this with Sienna Miller in *Layer Cake* were to become an integral part of his 'day at the office'.

5

HOLLYWOOD BECKONS

While Daniel had realised that movies were definitely the direction

in which he wanted his career to go, he was still canny enough to

recognise a quality television project when he saw one.

Thus it was in 2001 that the nation got to see him dazzle on the small screen in *Sword Of Honour*. William Boyd, writer/director of *The Trench*, adapted Evelyn Waugh's autobiographical trilogy into four hours of television. While Daniel triumphs in the lead role of Guy Crouchback, he was initially suspicious when approached about the part by director Bill Anderson. 'When I went to meet the director I said, "If this is anything like Brideshead, f*** off. I can't be bothered with it." He just went, "No, we're not going to do that."'

A startlingly direct approach for any actor to take, Daniel was obviously desperate not to have to grow the floppy fringe he had adopted to try to win work when he left drama school. Set during the Second World War, *Sword* follows the journey of middle-aged failure Crouchback, who joins up in an attempt to make some sense out of his life. What he finds in the British Army horrifies him.

Not an immediately sympathetic character, viewers have to work hard to identify with Crouchback. This was something that Daniel welcomed: 'That's what makes him interesting. The fact that he is a bit of a screw-up. That either endears you to him, or you wish he'd get on with things. But I related to that, that's quite a modern feeling, that feeling that life ends up passing you by if you don't stop and think about it, but he forces himself in the wrong way: he thinks he's going to find it by going to war.'

The critic from *The Mail On Sunday* declared him 'magnificent' in the role, going on to add that he 'is fast becoming one of our finest screen presences'. As well as heightened profile and critical praise, his appearance in *Sword* had another unexpected benefit. Writer Patrick Marber was apparently watching TV with director Sam Mendes and informed him that Daniel Craig was exactly who he needed to cast as Hollywood legend Paul Newman's son in *Road To Perdition*. And so it came to pass, but not before another Hollywood

outing designed to raise his profile worldwide.

Based on an insanely popular video game, *Lara Croft: Tomb Raider*, starring Angelina Jolie, was meant to take the concept of Tomb Raider and elevate it to the level of an action adventure movie. For an actor who had prided himself on choosing interesting, quirky projects, *Lara Croft* was a calculated risk. It didn't fit in with his normal criteria for choosing projects, but it was going to get him some much-needed worldwide attention.

In an interview he gave to *The Guardian* while in production with the film, he sounded a little defensive. 'The deal is: I know about the game, I find out this guy Simon West is directing it; I get an interview to meet the guy and I really like him. I don't want to be screwed around and I think I'm going to play the poor English cousin in this big old movie. But my profile had been raised because of *Love Is The Devil*, and they were going, "We WANT YOU to do this movie" and for an actor that's "Oh, you do? Really?" It was shit or get off the pot time. I mean, I want to make smaller budget movies, much more character-based, with more of a message. But if I can do this movie and it can raise my profile enough...'

Daniel played Alex West, who appeared to be an old flame of Lara's who had gone over to the bad guys. His role was small and ill-defined, though Jolie did later claim that he was 'one of the best kissers' she'd ever worked with. While the film did great box office, it was deemed a turkey by critics.

While Daniel claimed to enjoy the travel involved, shooting took place in both Cambodia and Iceland, he was never comfortable on set. In an interview in *Arena* magazine in 2006 he confided: 'It was a lesson for me to see a film like that made. I've always felt one of the problems is if you start a project and there's not a good script or it's not in good shape you are going to be battling against it. I don't believe you should be rewriting scenes as you're going along. I could just never get

my head around what was supposed to be going on. I felt like a bit of a spare prick at a wedding throughout. And I probably looked like one, too.'

It was a lesson learnt for Daniel and, luckily for him, his next film was an entirely different and altogether more rewarding experience.

British theatre director Sam Mendes, now married to actress Kate Winslet, had hit Hollywood gold when he directed *American Beauty*. The film, starring Kevin Spacey, netted five Oscars, including one for best director. His next project, eagerly awaited by audiences and critics alike, was *Road To Perdition*. Set in the early 1930s,

Above: Daniel as German scientist 'Werner Heisenberg' in BBC4's *Copenhagen*.

Right: Director Simon West and cast members Iain Glen, Angelina Jolie and Daniel Craig attending the premiere of *Lara Croft: Tomb Raider* in Los Angeles.

it was a bleak and gritty gangster movie starring legendary actor Paul Newman and audience favourite Tom Hanks.

Mendes was having trouble casting Newman's son, Connor Rooney, as he wanted someone whose eyes could measure up to Newman's famous baby blues. Daniel explained what happened in an interview with *The Sunday Times*: 'The story goes that he (Sam Mendes) was watching television with Patrick Marber, and *Sword Of Honour* was on. Apparently, Marber said: "That's who you want for Connor".

'So Sam got me in the following day and basically told me I was doing this film. Then he told me the story and I thought, "F***ing great". And when he said, "I've got Tom Hanks, and Paul Newman's playing your dad," I said, "Don't tell me

any more, because I can't cope with this."'

The next thing he knew, Daniel was in Chicago having dinner with his famous co-stars, including Newman, Hanks and Jennifer Jason Leigh. Hardly believing his luck, or the stellar company he was keeping, he recalls having to force himself to be calm: 'I just had to stop myself drinking really heavily. I was sort of controlling my beer intake.'

Working on such a big-budget, heavy-weight movie was a turning point for Daniel. As he recalled afterward: 'When I went and did *Road To Perdition*, it was just like "F***. This is what I want to be doing."'

His role was that of the weak-willed and violent son of mob boss Newman's John Rooney. Desperately jealous of his father's right hand man and hitman Michael Sullivan (Hanks), his reckless actions lead

to danger for all concerned. He eventually meetshis end suffering a humiliating execution in a bath tub.

Obviously a huge fan of Newman, Daniel recalls behaving like a star-struck kid on set. He even asked him whether he'd eaten all the boiled eggs in the famous scene in *Cool Hand Luke*. The answer was apparently 'no'. 'But I mean, he's 76 now and doesn't want all this crap,' said Craig back in 2002. 'He tried to talk to me about cars. I have a car, I just don't drive it at 250mph, it's not really my deal. But he's chilled. He tells dirty jokes all the time – and I just had to match him with dirty jokes. That was our dialogue.'

Generally critically well received and a modest box office success, *Road To Perdition* was an excellent building block in Daniel's career. Although pleased

with the film, Daniel decided that he didn't want to try and capitalise on it by knocking down doors in Hollywood. 'I think the film is great, I think I get away with it. Good directors will watch something like that and they'll clock it and put it in their bank,' he told *The Sunday Times*. 'But it just doesn't happen immediately. There's that thing in America that I should go and hustle my arse and ride this wave, but I've just never done that and don't see why I should start now.' It was an interesting attitude for an apparently ambitious actor to take. Rather than 'hustling his arse' as he so delicately put it, he preferred to sit back and wait for the chances to come to him.

Of his three other projects that appeared in 2002, none was likely to have been seen by eager Hollywood casting directors. Cast

Above: Daniel could hardly believe his luck at being offered the chance to star alongside Tom Hanks and movie legend Paul Newman.

Above: In playing the weak-willed son of Paul Newman, Daniel was helped by his eyes matching the colour of Newman's famous baby blues.

as an astronaut in a ten-minute segment of art film *10 Minutes Older: The Cello*, he co-starred with former singer with the Fine Young Cannibals, Roland Gift.

Set in 2146, the short was directed by Michael Radford and saw Daniel's character, Cecil Thomas, age only ten minutes while the world has moved on by eighty years. This was a curiosity that was seen by a very limited number of arthouse film fans. He also appeared in the short *Occasional, Strong* as a gangster with a distinctly dodgy cod Cockney accent. This slight tale, directed by Steve Green, featured a gang out on a shooting

spree whose driver wins the lottery then loses the ticket. Reminiscent of *Lock, Stock And Two Smoking Barrels*, it had little to recommend it.

Far more serious was *Copenhagen*, a film made for the newly-launched channel BBC4. Based on a Michael Frayn play that had premiered at the National Theatre in 1998, it told the story of the friendship, and falling out, of two nuclear physicists. In yet another Nazi role, Daniel played Werner Heisenberg, the head of Nazi Germany's atomic energy programme. Stephen Rea played fellow scientist and former friend, the Danish Niels Bohr.

While it garnered a tiny audience, no surprise given the channel on which it aired, it was widely praised. The critic in *The Sunday Telegraph* described it as a 'real treat' and went on to say: '… it was flawlessly constructed, constantly unsettling and deeply moving, with wonderfully judged performances from Stephen Rea, Daniel Craig and Francesca Annis'.

Daniel's next film, *The Mother*, which came out in 2003, was to garner him a lot more attention. Directed by Roger Michell, the man behind hit British comedy *Notting Hill* from a script by Hanif Kureishi, the movie featured a love affair between a young man and a much older woman.

Daniel played Darren, a carpenter working on the house of his best friend Bobby (Steven Mackintosh), who ends up in a sexual relationship with Bobby's recently widowed mother. The plot is further complicated by the fact that he is also in a relationship with Bobby's sister Paula (Cathryn Bradshaw). Veteran British actress Anne Reid plays May, the mother of the title and is brilliant as an older woman who still harbours sexual and emotional longings. She had started her career on long-running British soap

Above: *Ten Minutes Older: The Cello* saw Daniel playing an astronaut who has aged just ten minutes while the rest of the world had moved on by eighty years.

Above: Daniel with
Anne Reid in *The
Mother.*

opera *Coronation Street* as Ken Barlow's wife Valerie Tatlock. Other screen credits included Victoria Wood's BBC sitcom *Dinnerladies* and classic comedy *Hancock's Half Hour*.

The film, while having a well-developed emotional base, also featured graphic sex scenes between Darren and May. This 'May to December' relationship shocked some and became a major talking point. In an interview with *GQ* magazine in 2004, Daniel dealt with this delicate issue in typical forthright fashion. 'I think one of the whole points of the movie is that we have to deal with the fact that old people like to f*** and if you don't think that's true, you're living in a fool's paradise.'

He did find the situation of having to simulate sex with someone old enough to be his mother to be a little uncomfortable at times, however: 'It was bizarre having to do quite graphic sex scenes with an older woman. For me that was a great acting experience to do. And Annie was brilliant with it. You are trying to portray something that is going to make an impact. You are trying to say that these people are getting very intimate. When you do it of course it's the coldest room, there's people standing around, it's always a difficult situation to get into.'

The film may have dealt with serious issues in a way that proved quite shocking, but Daniel also felt that it had its bleakly humorous side. He told *The Independent*: 'I think *The Mother*'s very funny, but that's just me. At the first cast and crew screening, a few people went, "Wow, this is a bit serious…" And then we took it to Cannes and they started laughing from the word go,

because it's horribly dark and funny. And I thought, "Yes, we've got them!"'

If his aim was to be noticed in films that were worthwhile, then *The Mother* had achieved that in spades. His next project was to do the same. Released in 2004, *Sylvia* was the biopic of poet Sylvia Plath in which he played her philandering poet husband, Ted Hughes.

His leading lady in this was none other than Gwyneth Paltrow, by that time a big Hollywood name having starred in films as diverse as *Shakespeare In Love*, *The Talented Mr Ripley* and *Sliding Doors*. Daniel recalls meeting her in the glamorous environs of the Hotel Cipriani in Venice: 'So grand isn't it? I mean f***ing hell! The world's gone mad. I literally met her for five minutes. I said, "Hello, let's make this good."'

Based on the real relationship between Plath and Hughes, the film shows how they meet at Cambridge University, get married, have children and how their relationship eventually falls apart. She committed suicide by putting her head in a gas oven, an event that is also depicted towards the end of the film.

At the time, Daniel admitted that he did have some qualms about playing such a controversial figure. A former Poet Laureate, Hughes had died in 1998, just a few years before the film was made. Daniel told *The Observer*: 'There's quite a bit of pressure riding on it. And also just the whole shit that goes with it – you know, the hatred directed at Ted Hughes. People are still scrawling 'pig' on his grave.'

Many people had blamed Hughes for Plath's untimely death, but he felt

Above: Daniel as 'Darren', adopting the suitably haunted look of a man who's having sex with his best friend's mother.

Above: Despite the serious issues dealt with in *The Mother*, Daniel found the film to be 'horribly dark and funny', as did its first audiences at Cannes. **Opposite:** Daniel punting with Gwyneth Paltrow in *Sylvia*.

that it was important not to judge their relationship: 'Ultimately within a relationship there's an unknown, which is just about those two people. You know, when you have friends who split up, the worst thing you can do is get involved.'

Because it was based on real events, *Sylvia* came in for a fair bit of criticism for departing from reality. It received very mixed reviews but *The Independent On Sunday* noted that Daniel was 'commanding' as Hughes, while Joe Queenan in *The Guardian* commented that Hughes was 'played with verve and dash by Daniel Craig, who resembles the young Richard Burton.'

Daniel's next film was again directed by Roger Michell, who had helmed *The Mother*. Based on the novel by Ian McEwan, *Enduring Love* started with a tragic accident involving a hot air balloon. Daniel plays Joe, a man who witnesses the accident while on a picnic with his girlfriend Claire (Samantha Morton). Also present is Jed (Rhys Ifans) who goes on to develop an unhealthy obsession with Joe that turns into stalking as he believes that God has brought them together.

While this was a serious film, Daniel was very funny on the subject of having to lock lips with his co-star Rhys Ifans. 'He had these teeth in that were broken and I

could feel them in his mouth and we'd be going for it and Roger would never shout cut, the bastard…'

A psychological thriller, *Enduring Love* again received very mixed reviews. The critic in *The Evening Standard*, however, was very complimentary about both Daniel and Rhys Ifans' performances, giving great credit to the director: 'Both Craig and Ifans get every help from Michell, who knows how to orchestrate performances, and neither has ever been better.' Ifans had worked with Michell before on *Notting Hill*, which might have explained that rapport. Michell has also been very complimentary about Daniel's skills: 'There's a strange paradox in Daniel. He's kind and gentle and lovable, and at the same time there's a simmering lunacy

just below the surface, something bad and dangerous. That's what makes him intriguing to watch.'

Daniel was able to showcase his 'badness' in his final film of 2004. Playing a nameless character, simply referred to in the credits as 'XXXX', Daniel dominated the stylish crime movie *Layer Cake*.

Directed by the producer of *Lock Stock And Two Smoking Barrels*, Matthew Vaughn, *Layer Cake* could just have been another bad copy of the aforementioned London gangster flick. It was saved, however, by a good script, its largely understated take on events and an excellent cast. Daniel played a middle-class cocaine dealer. All smart suits and low-key charm, it was an unflashy portrayal of a businessman whose trade

Opposite: Playing 'Ted Hughes', Daniel was surprised by adverse feelings that the former Poet Laureate could inspire amongst the general public.
Above: *Sylvia* told the story of the relationship between Ted Hughes and Sylvia Plath from their first meeting at university in Cambridge to her untimely suicide.

happened to be in illegal substances. As writer Will Self put it in *The Evening Standard*: 'Given troubling life by Craig, he becomes at once intense and diffident, with a charming arrogance that shades imperceptibly into rank immorality.'

The subtlety of his performance was widely admired and in *Layer Cake* he had found a vehicle as a leading man that allowed him to demonstrate both his toughness and his vulnerability. As director Matthew Vaughn put it: 'What he doesn't do on screen is as important as what he does. Brave actors are the people who look like they're doing nothing, and they you cut it all together and there's a hell of a performance.'

When asked later whether it was a role that opened doors, he explained: 'I guess so. I'd been offered gangster films – or crime movies, because I'd say *Layer Cake* is more of a crime film than it is a gangster

movie – and none of them appealed to me; scripts with huge amounts of violence in them, with supposedly scary people, but whom I don't find scary. But what was different about that movie was its intelligent through line. I think it's very close to the truth, it's what successful drug dealers are like. They don't drive around in flashy cars, they don't show off, they behave quietly.'

So, despite his diffidence at knocking down doors and begging for big roles, doors were certainly beginning to open. The following year would see him show up in a much-talked-about Steven Spielberg project and rumours were already starting to circulate that a certain secret agent might just be within his grasp. Other names touted for Bond in 2004 included Eric Bana, Clive Owen, Hugh Jackman and Ewan McGregor. It seemed that, at least for now, the field was wide open.

6

TAKING AIM AT BOND

While the official announcement that Daniel Craig would be

the new James Bond wasn't made until 15 October 2005,

rumours had started to circulate more than a year before.

Of course, Daniel's name wasn't the only one being bandied about – Australian Eric Bana who had starred in *Troy* alongside Brad Pitt, Scottish favourite Ewan McGregor and the urbane and very English Clive Owen were among other candidates mentioned. It was only much later, once the role was secured, that Daniel admitted that he'd been in talks with Eon Productions, the makers of Bond, since 2004. Invited to a meeting in their offices in Piccadilly by co-producers Barbara Broccoli and Michael G Wilson, Daniel was initially reluctant even to consider the role.

'A lot of people were saying, "Oh my God, well, here's the golden ticket." I couldn't look at it like that. It's a poisoned chalice if it doesn't work out properly.'

Three months went by and he told them he wasn't interested. An apparently determined Broccoli set up another meeting. As Daniel told American magazine *Premiere*: 'I said, "Look, until I read a script I cannot even begin to…" and that was already me with one foot in the door.'

But a lot was to happen before he was finally to be cast and the world was to learn that he'd taken the role. As befits a canny actor on the rise, he was busy shooting a whole range of projects designed to cement his screen presence. The first the public was to see of him in 2005 was in an increasingly rare television appearance. Based on the best-selling novel of the same name by Robert Harris, *Archangel* was a three-part drama for the BBC.

Scripted by Dick Clement and Ian La Frenais, best known for their classic sitcom *Porridge* and comedy drama *Auf Wiedersehen, Pet*, it starred Daniel as Oxford academic Fluke Kelso. After delivering a lecture at a conference in Moscow, he becomes embroiled in a chase to track down Communist dictator Josef Stalin's missing diary. An intriguing and high quality TV drama shot in Russia

and Latvia, Daniel clearly thought that *Archangel* would do his burgeoning film career no harm. As the star of the piece, he received a lot of positive attention and excelled as the womanising, slightly down-at-heel academic.

His next role was in the wildly different film *The Jacket*, released in the UK in May 2005. Reunited professionally with his friend John Maybury, the man who had directed him in *Love Is The Devil*, he took a small part as a mentally ill man locked up in an institution. The film's lead was Adrien Brody who had won an Oscar for his role in Roman Polanski's *The Pianist*. He played Jack, a Gulf War veteran who finds himself wrongly convicted of a murder and ends up in a strange rural institution along with Daniel's character Rudy McKenzie.

Rudy tries to warn Jack about the torture that goes on, as hospital staff lock up the inmates in tiny confined, morgue-like boxes. Asked about being the only truly 'mad' person in the film, Daniel told *Empire*: 'Well, the only speaking-part mad person! There are lots of dribblers in there too, you'll notice. I think he's less mad than he makes out to be. I think he's sick and troubled and he's been tortured. He's been put through the mill, so I think his rambling is more about keeping people at a distance than him being genuinely mad.'

Daniel is convincingly scary and with lines like 'The four horsemen of the apocalypse are coming to see me today and they're not bringing flowers,' someone you'd definitely want to avoid. With his hair dyed black and not a great deal of screen time, *The Jacket* was not a film to establish his leading man credentials. But it did fit with his quest not always to go for the obvious roles. As he later explained: 'I have to say, there's always been a conscious decision with me to look for the more challenging roles. Money is an important consideration of course, but since *Our Friends* I knew that the pressure was off, I realised that for a while I could look for the best roles that I could. I know it's

Opposite: Daniel with one of his co-stars from *The Jacket*, Keira Knightley, at the movie's London premiere in May 2005.

a cliché, but it's about making the next thing you do better than the last. Also it's a question of not looking at normal things, trying to do the odd and unusual things.'

Between his being announced as Bond and his unveiling in *Casino Royale*, there were to be three films in which the public could judge his suitability for the part. Cries of outrage had greeted his casting as 007 and the press were looking for any excuse to bring him down.

They would find little to criticise in *Munich*, Steven Spielberg's long-awaited film about the aftermath of the shooting of Israeli athletes at the Munich Olympic Games in 1972. When Daniel was first approached about appearing in a pet project of one of Hollywood's most powerful men, he was incredulous. 'I just got a call to go and see him in Paris. And I did. I didn't f***ing believe it because they were being so secretive. I thought it was a f***ing joke. I thought I'd get there and they'd say, "It's f***ing Stefan Spielman, mate. Porn producer." He basically said, "I'd like you to do this, I'd like you to get involved."'

For any actor, such an offer from Spielberg would be an incredible honour. For Daniel, it was a major and unexpected

Caption: Eric Bana
and Daniel accompany
Steven Spielberg to a
screening of *Munich* in
Los Angeles.

breakthrough. When asked what it was
like to come out of such a meeting, he
said: 'You go out and spend lots of money.
I think I went and had a couple of beers.
I had that situation when I went to see
Sam Mendes for *Road To Perdition*. I was
about to get on a plane, so I went to the
bar and said, "Two beers and whiskies
and two more after that," and just went
bang, bang, bang. The barman said, "Are
you celebrating something?" I said, "I
can't tell you what I'm celebrating, but

I will after four of these. Guess what?"'
Such enthusiasm is endearing and shows
that Daniel was far from blasé about his
burgeoning career.

Munich was a serious film about a
serious subject. When 11 Israeli athletes
were murdered at the 1972 Olympic
Games by Palestinian terrorists, the world
looked on in horror. Israel then went on to
form a secret assassination squad whose
mission was to kill eleven Palestinian
targets in Europe.

Described as being 'inspired by real events', the film tracks the actions of the, at times, very amateurish group of men. Daniel plays Steve, an Afrikaans member of the squad who was the most gung-ho among the men.

His co-stars include Eric Bana and Ciaran Hinds. As his character remarks in the film: 'I'm the only one who actually wants to shoot these guys.'

Designed to show the ongoing horror of vengeance, Spielberg described the movie as 'a prayer for peace'. Daniel explained: 'The movie is about revenge, and you get to see how revenge works and how it's completely cyclical. You can compare it to the Northern Ireland conflict or take it back to Oliver Cromwell if you really want to. The only way to end a crisis like this is to start talking, and not just on a civilian level but at the highest level possible and until that happens there will be continual violence. I believe that human beings really do want to live in peace.'

Above: Marcell Nagy as a concentration camp victim and Daniel as an American soldier in *Fateless*.

He also describes going out for drinks with Israeli and Palestinian actors from the film, a small event that he believes may have led to better understanding. 'When we were shooting the Beirut scene we had young Palestinian actors and young Israeli actors and at the end of the day we all went out for a drink together. It was actually very moving because the guys said, "We would never get to meet usually". Despite being geographically very close they were worlds apart. Even on a small, but poignant level I thought, "there's something the movie's done before we've even finished it." I'm just proud to be part of it, as an actor it's part of the job to do things that tackle the difficult questions.'

Daniel Craig fans had two more chances to catch his work before the world premiere of *Casino Royale*, though both were rather hard to spot. He had only a handful of scenes in *Sorstalansag* aka

Fateless, a Hungarian film set during the Second World War. Playing an unnamed American soldier who was kind to the film's central character, a young Jewish boy caught up in the Holocaust, he appears very briefly in the film that was released in the UK in May 2006.

And it was only his voice that could be heard in *Renaissance*, a French animated movie made in 3D. Set in Paris in 2054, it tells the tale of a policeman bent on tracking down a missing scientist. He voices Barthelemy Karas, the aforementioned cop. Both of these projects would certainly qualify under his 'odd and unusual' criteria while doing little to distract from what was to be the main event of that year and, indeed, his career with the release of the highly anticipated twenty-second Bond movie. There were, however, many storms to weather before that triumphant moment.

THE ADVENTURE BEGINS

When Daniel Craig finally got the phone call that confirmed his life was

about to change forever, he was in the midst of the very unglamorous

activity of food shopping.

Having had several meetings with the Bond producers, and screen tested along with four other actors, he knew that the final decision could send his life in a very different direction. During a break from filming sci-fi thriller *The Invasion* in Baltimore with Nicole Kidman, his mobile rang in the middle of a branch of the posh food chain Whole Foods. The exact words of Bond supremo Barbara Broccoli? 'Over to you kiddo'.

'It's kind of sad', he told American magazine *Premiere*. 'I think the story's rather sad that I wasn't on a yacht in the middle of the Mediterranean when, "Hello darling, you're Bond" came through. I was in a f***ing Whole Foods. The irony of the Whole Foods story, for me, is great. It makes everything else real.'

Daniel has told how he abandoned his groceries, went to the nearest liquor store, bought some vodka, vermouth and a cocktail shaker and went home and had a few martinis. It was the obvious and natural reaction for someone who's just been told they're going to become the world's favourite spy. After having gone through the meetings with the Bond team and the auditions, he had already decided to take the job if it was offered. But the prospect of assuming the mantle of this famous screen icon was something with which he had struggled.

Worries about future typecasting, not being able to get the unusual roles he had built his career upon and damaging his 'brand' had all gone through his head. Unsure of the impact his decision would have, he confessed to asking for the opinions of everyone he knew, and even some he didn't. He told *GQ* in a December 2006 interview: 'I asked everybody. Passers-by, the lot. "Hello mate, can I talk to you about James Bond?" "Will you f*** off? Lunatic!" I asked Steven Spielberg. I said, "Would you employ me again if I did Bond?" He said, "course I f***ing would". Well, not quite with that accent. Or that profanity. But he's a huge Bond fan. I asked everybody. It divided my friends a bit. Some of them said, "You're gonna f*** yourself here." And they might be right. All I can say is, if I'd said no, I would be spitting now, having seen the process go through and knowing what I know now."

His doubts were somewhat assuaged once he had read the script. Originally penned by Neal Purvis and Robert Wade, it was given a rewrite by Paul Haggis, the man behind Oscar-winning film *Crash*. 'It read brilliantly,' said Daniel. 'It read like something that was being absolutely reverential toward the history of Bond but was also taking the piss out of all the Bonds. And I got that cold bead of sweat down my forehead, going, "Oh shit." So we moved along with it.'

He also realised that being known worldwide as James Bond might not necessarily be a bad thing, telling the *Daily Telegraph*: 'I hope it's going to be liberating. I'm not putting any negative spin on this because to be typecast as James Bond is a very high-class problem for an actor, and I'm certainly going to try and get as much out of it as I can. Of course, I am always going to think about whether it is going to limit what I do. I plan for it not to, but if it does, I'll approach that problem when it comes.'

The director of *Casino Royale*, Martin Campbell, wasn't initially enthusiastic about casting Daniel and took his time making the decision. He told *Premiere*: 'I wasn't totally convinced about Daniel. I was still thinking inside the old box. (Daniel's) obviously a terrific actor, a very interesting looking guy. He's got a toughness to him. But it was when Paul Haggis came on to do the rewrite that it all fell into place. It became a more serious Bond, a more realistic Bond. Much more like the books. And then, of course, Daniel fits perfectly.'

The woman who championed Daniel from the very beginning was Barbara Broccoli. The daughter of the famous Bond producer Albert R Broccoli, she co-produces the movies with her half brother Michael G Wilson. It was widely

Previous spread: Daniel treated himself to a few vodka martinis when he learned that he had landed the role of the new 'James Bond'.
Opposite: A *Casino Royale* movie poster as it appeared in Japan.

Below: Daniel and Nicole Kidman face the press at a conference prior to the filming of *The Invasion*.

EL CRAIG

NICOLE KIDMAN

reported that in a leaked memo from Eon Productions, the company behind the Bond franchise, Eric Bana was considered not handsome enough, Hugh Jackman was too fey, Ewan McGregor too short and Colin Farrell too sleazy. It was Daniel that Ms Broccoli thought perfect all along.

Her quote in *The Sunday Times* in October 2006 would certainly seem to bear this out. 'We live here. We are familiar with the actors here. I saw Daniel in *Our Friends In The North*. I saw him in *Elizabeth*, just walking down the hallway. I thought, "My God." He does have extraordinary presence. Just look at the body of work. He can be a character actor but he can also be a leading man. And a star. It's a pretty unique thing. He seemed the obvious choice. And he has surpassed our expectations.'

Opposite: Daniel poses at the 'Bond 21' press call aboard HMS *President* on the Thames in London.
Above: Daniel with *Casino Royale* director Martin Campbell.

If Ms Broccoli was at all swayed by the press, she would have had cause to question her decision when Daniel's casting was announced on 14 October 2005. In retrospect, the staging of the press conference could have been a bit better thought out, although no-one involved could have predicted quite what a vitriolic reaction Daniel's casting as Bond was going to provoke.

When Daniel set off down the Thames on 14 October, on a speedboat or 'rigid raider' craft with two members of the Royal Marines, he knew he was in for some tough questioning. His relationship with the press had been a prickly one since the tabloids had covered both his brief relationship with supermodel Kate Moss and an alleged fling with his *Layer Cake* co-star Sienna Miller. Turning up looking grumpy and wearing a life jacket over his suit didn't help matters. The press used the presence of the life jacket to imply that he was too wimpy to play Bond. The fact that he announced: 'I'd like to thank the Royal Marines for bringing me in like that – and scaring the shit out of me,' just played into their hands.

He looked uneasy at the press conference on board HMS *President*. It was obviously difficult to field questions about the new film, and what he was going to bring to Bond, as he had not yet started shooting *Casino Royale*. And when asked cheekily whom he'd prefer as a Bond girl, Sienna Miller or Kate Moss, he simply said: 'I'm not going to get into that.'

The headlines the next day did not bode well. 'The Name's Bland, James Bland' and 'It's Double-0 Dishevelled!' were typical. Strangely proprietorial about the British secret agent, it seemed that the press had

decided that Daniel was simply not the man for the job.

Fans of Bond, also a typically passionate lot, soon joined in. A website appeared – craignotbond.com – designed to make their displeasure known at Daniel's casting. Criticised for being too blond, not handsome enough and too short to play our national hero, it was proposed that fans should boycott *Casino Royale* simply because Daniel was in it. As one posting on the website had it: 'How can an actor with the rough face of a professional boxer and a penchant for playing killers, cranks,

Above: Eon producers Michael G Wilson and Barbara Broccoli with Daniel and Martin Campbell, joking with the press.

cads and gigolos pull off the role of the tall, dark, handsome and suave secret agent?'

By the time the website was widely publicised, Daniel was already on location shooting the film. He confessed afterwards that the criticism bothered him, likening it to school playground bullying. As he told American *Esquire* magazine: 'You lose your sense of humour very rapidly. I remember when the shit hit the fan on the Internet. We were in the Bahamas, working really hard.

'Then you read this stuff. I had a very dark two or three days. I was very despondent. But I realised I was peeing into the wind. I vowed to work twice as hard and get it right. Get it *beyond* right.'

When asked later about tabloid claims that he'd actually been seasick on the speed boat on the way to the press conference, he was equally vehement: 'You know, normally I wouldn't answer these questions, but f*** it, no I didn't get queasy on that boat. Some of the stuff that's been said is as close to playground taunts as you're going to get. "You've got big ears"… f***ing hell! But it's not right. Ask anyone who's been bullied… it hurts. There's a part of me that would love to turn around and shove it up their arse.'

He didn't know it at the time but, when the movie was eventually released, his critics would be forced to eat their words. In the meantime, like the true professional that he was, he swallowed it all and got on with the business of being Bond.

And there was absolutely no doubt that, having decided to take on the famous role, he treated it with the seriousness and reverence that it deserved. He admitted later that he watched the entire Bond back catalogue before stepping foot on set.

'I've got the box set,' he rather endearingly told *The Times*, 'and I went through them all religiously. Not so that I can answer a question at a press conference – although if you want to, test me! – but, you know, for tips. Some of

those are great movies and any film-maker would be lying if they said they didn't copy off people, because you have to. I just wanted to go through them all and there was stuff that Sean did and Roger (Moore) did and all of them did that were their little keys and you go, "oh, that's cute, they way they did that…" It's not something to do consciously, but just to have a mental note of.'

He admits that his favourite previous Bond, and the one he first saw on screen as a child, was Sean Connery. The Scottish actor became just about everyone's favourite Bond, but he wasn't without his critics when he was first cast in *Dr No* in 1962. Ian Fleming, the author of the original books, dismissed Connery as 'a snorting lorry driver' but that didn't stop Connery becoming synonymous with the author's suave spy.

'Sean Connery set and defined the character,' said Daniel. 'He did something extraordinary with that role. He was bad, sexy, animalistic and stylish, and it is because of him I am here today.' Daniel even went so far as to contact Connery after he was offered the role: 'I wanted Sean Connery's approval and he sent me messages of support, which meant a lot to me.' William Boyd, who had directed Daniel in *The Trench* also felt moved to compare him to Connery, saying that there was 'something about both men which is incredibly amiable and nice, but also strong and no-nonsense. Connery has that Scottish Calvinist aspect to him and maybe there is something like that in Daniel.'

It also reflects well on Daniel's character that he was determined to do the right by the previous Bond incumbent. Irish actor Pierce Brosnan had impressed as Bond in the four preceding films – *GoldenEye, Tomorrow Never Dies, The World Is Not Enough and Die Another Day*. But it was rumoured that he was being replaced because, at 52, he was too old.

Opposite: Arriving for the *Casino Royale* press call with the Royal Marines led to accusations that Daniel had been sea-sick aboard their boat. Following spread (left): Previous 'Bonds', including Roger Moore, lent their support to Daniel in the role. Following spread (right): Daniel was entirely open with Pierce Brosnan about the possibility of taking over the 'Bond' role from him.

Right: Daniel trained hard for the 'Bond' movies, mastering a number of new skills.
Opposite: Daniel posing with Eva Green at The One And Only Ocean Club in the Bahamas.

Running into Brosnan at the BAFTA awards in February 2005, even though he hadn't yet been offered the role, he decided to come clean. As he told *Premiere*: 'I didn't know how much he knew about this. But if I wasn't upfront with him about it, if I met him again I wouldn't be able to look him in the eye.' Telling him that it was a possibility, he asked him what he thought. 'I don't know if I gave him much choice but he said, "go for it". He didn't hit me. I don't know (if) anybody was underhanded with Pierce about this, but I know I wasn't.'

It seems that Brosnan was impressed with Daniel's honesty, and his acting skills, later saying: 'I think Daniel is a very fine actor. These are choppy waters and they're going to get him one way or another. But I think he will have the last laugh at the end of it.'

And Brosnan wasn't the only one stepping up to the plate to defend Daniel. His co-star in *Casino Royale*, much-loved actress Judi Dench, was fierce in her response to his detractors: 'I hate how people have been attacking Daniel Craig. It's despicable and it disgusts me. His critics will be proved wrong.'

Even before all the critics waded in, Daniel knew that he was going to have to be super fit if he was even going to consider taking to the screen as the daring spy. He later told *The Times*: 'I started training for the film when I knew there

was a possibility that I might get the part. And I though "f*** it, I'll start trying to get myself fit anyway and even if it doesn't come off I'll live another year". And if I hadn't done it, I don't think I would have survived.'

He wasn't super-serious about it, however, showing his human side when he admitted: 'But I'm not obsessive about it. I work out three or four times a week, but I take the weekends off and drink as much Guinness as I can get down my neck.'

If Daniel was nervous about the physical demands about to be placed on him, then so was director Martin Campbell. 'Daniel had never done an action film before and you gamble that he is going to be able to deal with that. Action is difficult. There's a tendency to be dismissive and say "Oh, it's just action…" But it's tricky. And I'm talking about the kind of action that feeds into the character and narrative, not the sequences that are there for their own sake. Some actors you might expect to be very good because of their image, turn out to be incapable of doing action.'

As they headed off to the first of many exotic locations, Daniel and Campbell were about to find out exactly what the new, super-fit Daniel Craig was actually capable of achieving.

8

BOND COMES TO LIFE

On 31 January 2006, principal photography began on *Casino Royale*, Bond 22. For its star, it was to be an incredible journey, geographically, physically and mentally. Locations were as diverse as the Czech Republic in sub zero temperatures to the canals of Venice, the famous Bond stage at Pinewood Studios, England and the gorgeous climate of the Bahamas.

Daniel knew that his task was an enormous one and that he had a lot to prove. Not only was he following in the footsteps of five other actors who had filled Bond's shoes, he had to take the character in a new and believable direction. He acknowledged the pressure to get things right in an interview he gave to *The Sun* while filming in the Bahamas: 'I know there are a lot of fans out there who James Bond is incredibly important to. I want to make it clear he is incredibly important to me as well. I am putting everything I can into this movie and we are putting in something else as well – an X factor we haven't seen before.'

Certainly producer Barbara Broccoli was keen to take Bond in a brand new direction. Famous for its unbelievable stunts and increasingly bizarre gadgets, she felt that this old formula had somewhat run out of steam.

As she explained to American magazine *Entertainment Weekly*: 'After the last film (*Die Another Day*), we spent eight months trying to come up with a story but just couldn't. The movies had become so fantastical – with invisible cars and stuff like that – there was just no way to continue in that same vein. There was nothing new left to do. So we decided to start all over with the story we've always wanted to tell – how Bond became Bond in the first place.'

The first book that author Ian Fleming wrote in the James Bond series, *Casino Royale* introduces us to the spy and tells of how he became a paid killer, albeit for the British government. Written in 1953, it is obviously a tome for its time and many things had to change to adapt it as a modern blockbuster.

Broccoli explained: 'We're going back to the character Ian Fleming originally conceived. It's not a period piece or anything like that. It's set today, right now, and it's got all the action fans have come to expect from the movies. But we're getting back to the essence of Bond, to the Bond in Fleming's first 007 novel.'

Caption: Daniel with Eva Green, who played 'Vesper Lynd' on the *Casino Royale* set in Loket near Carlsbad in the Czech Republic.

The 'double 0's refer to two kills and to become a 'double 0' agent, you need to have eliminated two targets. In the precredits sequence to *Casino Royale* we see Bond confront a colleague who taunts him for not being a 'double 0'. In flashback, we see Bond killing a man in a bathroom in a brutal and messy fashion and then shooting his colleague in cold blood. The message is clear, this is Bond from the

beginning and his job is not a pretty one.

Daniel commented afterwards: 'I watch that bathroom sequence and I wince. All my knuckles split, my hands were in bandages after it. And I had a fight double – Ben. I did the bits that hurt. And he did the bits that really f***ing hurt. But that's the thing with this Bond. He bleeds. It's more about the fact that he bleeds, goes down and gets up again.'

While this new Bond was decidedly more brutal, and less sympathetic, than the ones that came before, he also gave Daniel a chance to make his own mark on the character. Going back to the very beginning of Bond's story allowed the team working on *Casino Royale* to reinvent Bond in his own image.

Having read Fleming's original novel, Daniel was determined to incorporate some of its original grit into the role. 'There are elements that are important and it's crucial that we see them. What we get in this movie, as well as all the action that's gonna happen, is an incredibly complex story about how this man becomes who he is.'

He was also pleased that the final script reflected Fleming's chequered characterisation. 'What I like about this script is that we have a Bond who – at least at first - is sort of fallible and doesn't get it right, so therefore he has to learn. That's not saying that you should then forgive him for his bad behaviour, but you should sort of understand him. Because he's Bond. He's not always nice.'

In the original texts, and also in some of the early movies, Bond is also deeply sexist. This has been toned down so as not to jar too much with a modern audience but it is still in there. Daniel admits he was concerned about how that would play out: 'There's always been that unpleasant

Left: Crucial scenes for *Casino Royale* were shot in Venice, Italy.

side to Bond. Sean Connery used to smack women around the face in films. Some of that is still in there. I think it has to be. All I was interested in was finding out why Bond is like that. It's not that you can forgive him, but at least you go, "Oh, OK, I see why he behaves like that." If he seems to be morally corrupt, there's a reason for it, because ultimately he's getting paid to kill people.'

Obviously not wishing to be too unpleasant a character, he tried to negotiate a middle ground and portray a hero who is flawed: 'He is basically a dislikeable human being, and yet also incredibly likeable, because he is a rogue. That's the balance that I personally would like to try and strike with him.'

It was certainly important to Daniel that he looked the part of a man who was able to deal in casual violence. As he told a reporter from the *News Of The World*: 'I wanted to look like Bond could kill somebody. I'm not trying to be extra tough, but I wanted to look physically big. I got a personal trainer. I wanted to bulk up quickly so I did a lot of weights and had a high protein diet.'

The physical demands of carrying such a high-profile movie with such a high proportion of demanding stunts were also enormous, as he admitted to *Arena*. 'I'm working on it. It goes with the territory. I owe it to the character to make sure that physically he looks like he's done some of the things he says he's done. I'm just trying to get my head around being involved in every scene and in every action sequence. Of course it's Bond, but I want it to be as real as possible. I want to make people think, "Oh my God," rather than "Oh, I've seen it all before". I know it's a cliché but I want people to be on the edge of their seats.'

Right: 'Bond' and 'Vesper' arrive in Venice by yacht.

Previous spread: In an *homage* to Sean Connery's 'Bond', an Aston Martin of the kind introduced in *Goldfinger* made an appearance in *Casino Royale*.

Above: Daniel in the Brioni dinner suit that he described as 'a wondrous thing to behold.'

As if all the external pressure wasn't enough, he was obviously piling a lot of extra demands on himself in order to get the role just right. This included being as heavily involved as many as stunts as was humanly possible, despite his lack of experience in action movies.

He told the *Daily Telegraph*: 'I wanted to do as much of the action work as I could, so that the audience can see it's me and it's real. I feel like I became a sportsman of sorts, and that meant acquiring injuries and carrying on and bashing through to the next level of pain. Although the stunt team did fantastic work to make sure that everything was as safe as possible, if you

don't get bruised playing Bond, you're not doing it properly. I had black eyes, I had cuts, I was bruised, I had muscle strains, and I took a lot of painkillers. But it was part of the job. As much as I was hurt, the stuntmen were in much more pain.'

The stuntmen might indeed have been in more pain, but the film's stunt co-ordinator Gary Powell was mightily impressed with Daniel's efforts. 'Daniel really took some hits on *Casino Royale*. I'd see him bruised and cut up, fight after fight. And he'd just say, "Oh shit, that smarted a bit, let's go again." Pierce was a lovely man. But he'd always emerge from a punch-up or a huge explosion with

an unruffled tie and immaculate hair. Someone told me recently, "Sean Connery sweated, Roger Moore perspired and Pierce Brosnan glowed." I don't agree, but I'll add one thing – Daniel Craig bleeds. He did everything we asked of him and more.'

Unimpressed by Daniel's physical exertions, the British tabloid press were still looking for excuses to take pot shots at the new James Bond. As stories emerged of his various injuries sustained while filming, instead of taking these as examples of his physical courage, they tried to paint him as a wimp.

Much was made of the fact that he

had lost two teeth in a bloody fight scene filmed in Prague, and that his dentist had to be flown out for emergency surgery. The truth turned out to be rather more mundane. 'I got bumped and I knocked a crown out. I got it fixed, simple as that. It didn't hurt and there was no bleeding. I saw a dentist and never left the set. I completed the day's work. In James Bond movies, you are going to get hurt.'

One headline screamed 'Ow! Ow! 7' alongside a report that he'd developed prickly heat in the Bahamas. And the press went to town over a rumour that he couldn't drive a stick-shift car, only an automatic. How could someone so

Above: Although criticised in some quarters for not being tough enough, one of his trainers described Daniel as 'the only Bond who in real life could pass SAS selection.'.

incompetent be put in charge of Bond's famous Aston Martin, was the charge?

He put this latter rumour firmly to bed in an interview with *GQ*: 'Of course I can drive a manual car. I flogged the arse out of an Aston Martin DBS around Jeremy Clarkson's *Top Gear* track. And in the film I got the car up to 170mph. When I braked, we had those brakes just f***ing glowing. Will that do? Sorry but most posh cars are automatic. I think someone leaked that I drove one, which gets changed to "Ha, ha! You can't change gear!"'

The press also leapt on a quote given earlier in his career about hating handguns. It did seem rather ironic, given his latest role as Britain's most famous assassin. A man named Joss Skotowe, a gun expert who taught Daniel how to handle weapons for the film, came to his

Below: 'Bond' is floored by 'Solange' played by Italian actress Caterina Murino.

rescue, telling *The Sunday Mirror*: 'He came in hating guns but left rather keen. I've yet to meet a man who doesn't relish holding a Walther PPK. And Daniel is more man than most.

'We use real guns in the movie, even though they've been adapted to fire blanks. But blanks can still hurt or kill you. I brought in some SAS chums to give Daniel some extra training. And even they were impressed. One said to me, "that boy's a natural". And he's right. Daniel is the only Bond who in real life could pass SAS selection. He's fit, he looks like a killer and he's smart.

'I could never imagine Roger Moore or Pierce Brosnan doing any real damage to anything stronger than a vodka martini but Daniel could really hurt you, with or without a gun.'

The negative press stories, along with the online campaign to have him removed as Bond, only served to make him more determined to succeed. 'I always wanted to make a great movie but when things started happening online it gave me a resolve. It was like, "we've got no choice now – we have to make the best movie we can." In fact it spurred me on.'

Enough of his stunt work, what about his overall sex appeal? An alleged old school nickname, 'Potato Head', had been dug up by the press, while it was thought he was too short at 5ft 11in (1.77m) to be a convincing Bond. And then there was the blond hair. An American journalist reported that even a staff member at the hotel he was staying at had a definite opinion on Daniel's hair. He quoted him as saying: 'Seems like a nice fellow. Friendly. He'll do all right. He's blond you know? They'll dye his hair. Can't have him running around like *that* now can they?' It seems that they could, though, and he became blondest Bond in history.

But it was a scene in which he emerged from the sea wearing light blue swimming trunks that left little to the imagination that really sealed his place as the sexiest Bond ever. In a tribute to the famous scene in *Dr No* in which original Bond girl Ursula Andress emerged from the ocean in a skimpy white bikini, *Casino Royale* showcased Daniel as the buffest Bond yet. No wonder he felt compelled to spend time in the gym.

Daniel was well aware that it wasn't just Bond girls that were sex objects these days: 'The times change. That scene was a wink to Ursula Andress in *Dr No* who also played Vesper Lynd in the first *Casino Royale* in 1967. Four decades later and it's James who leaves the water in swimming trunks and attracts the looks.'

And he made sure he was involved in the decision-making when it came to exactly what he'd be wearing, too. 'The trunks were my choice. We sat with ten pairs on the table and discussed them at length. I mean, I just don't think Bond should wear Bermuda shorts. It's just not

right. Anyway, the ones I chose aren't that skimpy. I mean, they're not Speedos. That would have been wrong.'

And while Daniel does eventually slip on the famous Bond black tuxedo, it takes time to build up to this moment, as the film's costume designer, Lindy Hemming, explained. 'Daniel is a much more active type of hero, so I went with a far more action-style look. Everyone has this image of 007 as the dinner-jacketed hero but what we've tried to do in *Casino Royale* is build up to the idea of a man coming to look like James Bond. In the first part of the film, Bond is working undercover in Madagascar and he's dressed very casually, but by the time he meets Vesper Lynd on a train, he's beginning to look something like the 007 we all know. Bond's style is completely timeless.'

For those desperate for every sartorial detail, Daniel's tuxedo was tailor made by Brioni, the famous Milan-based fashion house and finished off with black ottoman silk trimmings, pure horn buttons and opaque grosgrain lapels. Daniel recalled, rather lovingly: 'A Brioni evening suit is a wondrous thing to behold. You put it on and it's like wearing silk gloves.'

It seems that the two Bond girls with whom he interacts were also pretty impressed with his sex appeal. Eva Green, who plays Vesper Lynd, said: 'Daniel is a super-sexy guy, a real man's man. He's also easy to work with.'

Caterina Murino who plays Solange, a woman he has a fling with in the early part of the movie was even more effusive: 'Our characters seduce each other and we are like animals. The sex scene is a bit strange but we looked at each other and we said, "let's do it". Unfortunately, it was very short. It was only one night. He is a great actor. He gives to this character something we never saw before. When he's going to kill someone, he looks like a real killer. When he kisses me, when he makes love, he's so sexy. You never saw a James Bond like this.'

You certainly never saw a James Bond suffer quite so graphically either. In a scene that appeared in the original

CASINO ROYALE

Above: Danish actor Mads Mikkelsen, who played the villain Le Chiffre, with Caterina Murino and Daniel at the Sony Center for the German premiere of *Casino Royale* in Berlin.

novel and was retained for the movie, Bond is tortured by villain Le Chiffre (Mads Mikkelsen) by being tied to a chair and having his genitals flayed from underneath.

It was a scene that had every male viewer wincing in sympathetic pain and was certainly a testing one for Daniel, as he wasn't afraid to admit. 'The bad guy takes the bottom out of a chair. I'm sat in it naked and supposedly my nuts are hanging down there, although I think in

that situation they would kind of go north. The bad guy gets a spliced piece of rope and he swings it under the chair and does me with it. It all has fibreglass protection but it did crack at one point and we stopped filming quite rapidly and I ran over the other side of the room. Woah!'

He said he prepared himself for the scene by getting himself angry: 'Bond thinks he's going to die. It's his last shout.' He manages to remain cool throughout, and his performance in this particularly

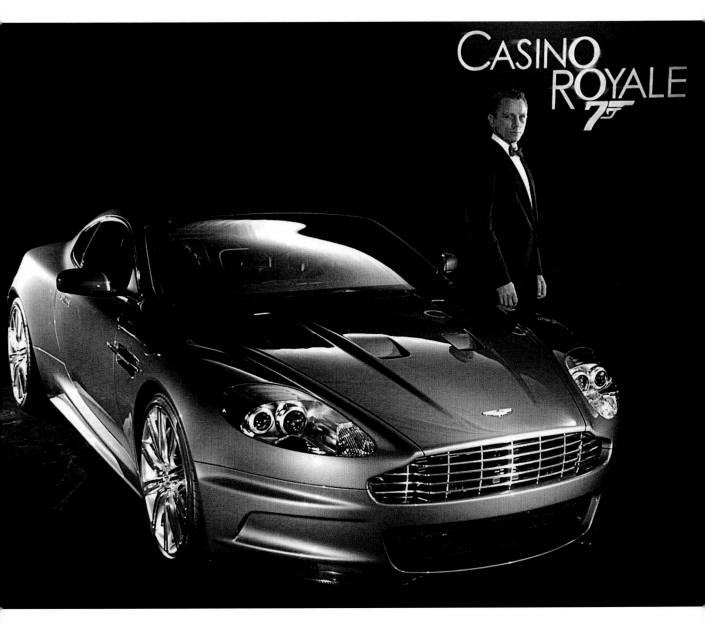

CASINO ROYALE 7

challenging scene convinced Barbara Broccoli, if she needed convincing, that she'd made exactly the right choice for her new leading man.

'Imagine a situation where your hero is captured and tied to a chair naked and having his genitals beaten…' she told the *Sunday Times*. 'How can he maintain the upper hand in that? Impossible, you would think. And you make it even harder for him by casting an extraordinary actor (Mads Mikkelsen) as the villain. Somehow,

the way Daniel does that scene, he comes out as the winner. It's hard to articulate what he does. But he does hold the power in that scene, and he does it throughout the movie. He has taken something that is really good on the page and made it better.'

While it would be easy to be cynical about a Bond producer talking up her leading man before anyone had seen the movie, the world was about to judge for itself as *Casino Royale* prepared to be released cinematically worldwide.

Above: The 21st century Aston Martin 'Bond' drove in *Casino Royale*.

9

LIFE AFTER BOND

When Daniel Craig braved the rain and the crowds at the world

premiere of *Casino Royale* on 14 November 2006, he still

didn't know what to expect. With long-term girlfriend

Satsuki Mitchell by his side, he smiled happily and obligingly

signed autographs for the waiting fans.

Previous spread:
Daniel as 'Perry Smith'
in Infamous.
Below: Some of
Daniel's greatest
detractors turned into
huge fans after their
first viewings of Casino
Royale.

Inside, an audience eager to see just what the brand new Bond looked like included a host of celebrities and Her Majesty The Queen. From the audience's reaction to the gritty, black and white opening sequence, it seemed clear that the reception for the new, darker Bond was going to be an overwhelmingly positive one. And so it was, as the critics fell over themselves to praise both the film and its star attraction. Daniel had beaten all the odds, silenced all his critics and delivered a compelling performance to become Britain's new favourite Bond.

Writing in *The Times*, critic Wendy Ide summarised the situation neatly: 'The immensely enjoyable *Casino Royale* answers its critics with an insouciant sneer and a self-confident swagger. The Craig naysayers are suddenly far less vocal as it becomes clear that the controversial casting is the best thing that's happened to the franchise in years. Craig brings a

brutally efficient physicality to the role and a thrilling undercurrent of sadistic cruelty – his is a Bond you feel gains real job satisfaction from his licence to kill.'

The Sun, a paper that had happily weighed into the Daniel-baiting the previous year, was punchier but no less effusive in its praise. 'The world's No1 secret agent blasts back onto our screens and Daniel Craig proves he's the best James Bond since Sean Connery. Daniel took a lot of flak when he landed the role, but he proves the doubters wrong as a new-look 007 packing enough attitude to power his famous Aston Martin car.'

Reading these reviews in the days that followed the film's premiere, Daniel can have been nothing less than delighted. Having weathered the storm of criticism that greeted his casting, as well as the seemingly endless stories about how he was too wimpy to ever be Bond, he had emerged triumphant. The temptation to tell his detractors to do something

quickly became the
most profitable 'Bond'
movie in the history of
the franchise.

anatomically impossible must have been overwhelming. But, as he told *The Times* a year later, he resisted the urge: 'Yes, when it came out and people liked it, believe me, there was no one happier. But I wasn't going to say, "f*** you". Because there was no need.'

Yes, gloriously positive headlines and acres of gushing praise in newsprint was probably reward enough. But, as with all movies, it is money taken at the box office that is the bottom line. Positive reviews help enormously but are not always enough. Producer Barbara Broccoli and Daniel had no need to worry. *Casino*

Royale had the biggest ever opening for a Bond film in Britain, grossing £13.4 million and topping the UK box office. And as word of mouth spread about the film's quality, the figures just kept getting better and better with the film raking in nearly £300m worldwide to make it the most profitable Bond film ever.

Daniel was in a hotel room in Switzerland when Barbara Broccoli rang to give him the good news. 'It was surreal. Just surreal. The numbers kept going up and up and up and it was like, "That's it! We've done it." When asked whether he'd cracked open some vintage champagne,

he seemed incredulous at such a question. 'You're joking aren't you? Champagne? No way. I had a couple of very large vodka martinis. I went to the bar and it was like, "Three please! Shaken, stirred or however you want to serve them."'

In a very human admission, he also confessed to letting it all hang out once filming on the extremely demanding *Casino Royale* had finished. 'After it finished, I stopped training. I got drunk for three months! No, I didn't, but I certainly relaxed for three months and ate what I wanted, and then it's hell because as soon as you get back in the gym, you

have to work all that off, and it takes much longer than it does to put it on.' However tough he might have been as Bond, it was nice to hear him being almost girlish in his struggles with his now famous figure.

He may have struggled with some conflict when it came to deciding whether or not to take on the famous role, but after the release and subsequent success of *Casino Royale* Daniel was much more sanguine about it. In fact, even during filming, he had realised that he simply had to make the most of the experience. When asked about his ambition to win Oscars, and how being Bond might frustrate that

Above: Although he knew he would never achieve his ambition of winning an Oscar while playing '007', Daniel decided just to 'Enjoy it.'

ambition, he told American *Esquire*: 'I mean, of course I want to win Oscars, every actor wants to win Oscars. But then it sunk in: if I don't take something like this when it comes around and have a go at it, then what? Yeah, there's gonna be negatives, but I've got to try to accentuate the… Ah, f***, it sounds like I'm gonna break into song any minute now. I figured, f*** it, it's Bond. Enjoy it!'

For someone who had been criticised by the British press for being po-faced, this was a refreshing attitude. He was a little perturbed by some people who took his portrayal of the British secret agent just a little too literally, though. He had this to say when asked about people's changing attitudes, post-Bond: 'The only thing that ever changes is some people suddenly think you're a multimillionaire. Some fans do think that I'm James Bond and that's even more worrying, and they write to me with plans of action. That is only a few I should say… Most people are very nice about it. You just have to keep your friends close.'

He reiterated this theme of keeping his friends close when asked if Bond had changed him, obviously keen to keep his feet on the ground: 'Nothing has changed yet. I have very good friends and a very close family. They'll keep a close eye on me and knock me back if I change too much.' It's a very British attitude for a very British spy – don't let success and fame go to your head, whatever happens. It's hard to imagine a Hollywood star expressing such sentiments.

If he was worried about typecasting, then the three films in which he starred that would come out the following year should have put paid to that. The first, *Infamous*, released in the UK on 19 January, 2007 was based on the character of American writer Truman Capote.

Rather overshadowed by the release of *Capote* another Truman Capote biopic the previous year, *Infamous* looked at what happened as the gay writer researched his famous book *In Cold Blood*. Daniel played Perry Smith, one of two men convicted of murdering a family in Kansas. With his hair dyed black and most of his scenes in a prison cell, this was very different material indeed to Bond. The film traces the developing relationship between Capote and Smith, with large hints of a repressed homosexual love affair between the two.

When asked about the erotic tension in the film, Daniel thought it realistic. 'There was never any self-consciousness about it. I always think that's how a love story needs to play out anyway, because it's just this friendship that starts growing, and if it turns into sex, it turns into sex; but it's not like two young men meet in a bar, go out back and f***. This is about two human beings really sitting down and trying to figure each other out.'

Toby Jones, the British actor who played Capote, was asked quite a few embarrassing questions about what it was like to kiss the new 007. Daniel found this both exasperating and highly amusing: 'What's he supposed to say? "Very dry?" Anyway, it's all over the internet now: "Bond has gay kiss!"'

His next film to be released in October 2007 was *The Invasion*. This was the film he was working on when he first found out he'd won the Bond role and co-starred big-name Hollywood actress Nicole Kidman. Loosely based on *The Invasion Of The Body Snatchers*, it told the tale of how a space shuttle crash led to the invasion of alien DNA. This flu-like virus turned normal humans into automatons. A piece of not very convincing sci-fi horror, it didn't wow critics or do great business at the box office. Daniel also had very little to do as Ben, a British scientist and sometime love interest of Kidman's character Carol.

Much more interesting was *The Golden Compass*, which came out in December 2007. Based on the first part of writer Philip Pullman's *His Dark Materials* trilogy, it was a fantastical story of parallel worlds where people's souls come alive as animals known as Daemons.

Daniel played Lord Asriel, an explorer and the uncle of the film's main character Lyra played by young English actress

Right: Daniel was reunited with Nicole Kidman in *The Golden Compass*.

Left: Daniel loved working with the youngsters on *The Golden Compass* but contributed more than anyone to the on-set swear box.

Dakota Blue Richards. It was a project he was extremely keen to sign himself up for. 'When I heard they were making the film I thought, "I'd like to do this". I am such a big Philip Pullman fan and his sort of philosophies, morals and the way he looks at the world. He writes children's stories but with major adult themes and ideas about being a good person and making the right choices.'

He even put himself forward for the role, something he had been reluctant to do in the past. 'I have no career masterplan at all. I read the books and was a big fan, so when I finished Bond I made the phone call. I knew one of the producers and they said the part was still open if I was interested. It just fitted in and I leapt at it.'

Along with Dakota, his co-stars included Nicole Kidman as baddie Mrs Coulter and *Casino Royale* Bond girl Eva Green as Serafina Pekkala, Queen of the Witches. It was the presence of Dakota that caused him the most problems on set though. Never one to censor his expletives, he ended up contributing a fortune to the swear box on set. 'It was worth the money but it cost me a small fortune. It became a joke after a while. Sometimes Dakota would be on set and you wouldn't know it and you'd hear, "It's another pound". But I get a big kick out of working with children because you've got to keep them enthused. Dakota learned quickly and I teased her a lot to get her energy level going so we could bounce off each other. It was a real pleasure.'

While the release of these three very different films showed the world, and casting directors, that he was capable of very different roles, there was one other appearance in 2007 that would seal his place in the hearts of the British public.

Showing that he did indeed have a sense of humour and wasn't the least bit afraid of taking the Mickey out of himself, he appeared on a Comic Relief sketch with British funny woman Catherine Tate. An annual event run and screened by the BBC and designed to raise money for charity,

Comic Relief gets big viewing figures as celebrities line up to do something that is usually out of character. And nothing could have been further from the suave image of James Bond than Daniel's appearance in the pre-recorded film for Comic Relief.

Catherine Tate had developed the character of Elaine Figgis in her award-winning sketch show *The Catherine Tate Show*. A middle-aged spinster from Yorkshire and an eternal optimist, Elaine's previous romances had been with a death row inmate from Texas and an Egyptian waiter who'd run off with her life savings. When she met BondBoy68 in an internet chat-room, they struck up a friendship over their shared love of Canadian crooner Celine Dion and soon he'd moved in.

Shot as a mockumentary, we cut to Daniel sitting in Elaine's very dowdy front room. Strangely though, she's not overly impressed with her new live-in lover, confiding to the camera: 'Well, he says he's an actor, but I've never heard of him. No, I think he works at Carphone Warehouse.'

Daniel, however, seems very much in love and totally at home. Occasionally getting up to make sandwiches with his favourite brand of brown sauce and slurp a bottle of Newcastle Brown Ale, he tells the film-makers: 'She doesn't know what I do, but she knows who I am.'

Things take a turn for the worse when they head off on a tandem for a camping holiday in Kirby Moorside. On their return we learn that she wanted to see the sights, but he wanted to stay in the tent and cuddle. His protestations of undying love are greeted with indifference by Elaine, who clearly has no idea that James Bond is in her living room attempting to plight his troth. 'Don't get me wrong,' she says. 'He's a lovely chap, but he's no John Nettles.'

Her preference for the (much older) actor and star of *Midsomer Murders* leads her to throw Daniel out on his ear, his teddy bear following a close second. Retaining a straight face

throughout, Daniel was wonderful as the
misunderstood heart-throb looking for
love with the dowdy spinster. One of the
highlights of that year's Comic Relief, it
showed him to be the best of sports and
was a daring departure for someone who
had strived so long to be taken seriously as
an actor.

Right: As a great Philip Pullman fan, Daniel leapt at the chance to play Lord Asriel in *The Golden Compass*.

10

THE PRICE OF FAME

Daniel Craig had long been of the opinion that a career as an actor

should not require him to reveal details of his personal life. With the

British press desperate for details about any celebrity's every move,

this was a tension that would increase as he became more famous.

One of his main hesitations when considering the role of Bond was that it would catapult him even further into the limelight. Daniel ultimately decided that the risk was worth it and that he would deal with each challenge as it arose.

Maybe he felt that the steady line that he had taken in the past would help him. When asked about keeping his private life private, he told *The Times* shortly before the release of *Casino Royale*: 'I've been consistent about that in the past and I don't see why it should change now. Obviously, I know that this job comes with a lot of scrutiny and a high profile and I'm more than happy to sit down and talk about the work, the filming, whatever. But I don't see why I should have to discuss the details of my private life in public.'

His ambivalence about such personal publicity partially explains why the tabloids were so keen to knock him down when the Bond announcement was made. Some journalists have dismissed Daniel as sullen and difficult, frustrated at his well-known unwillingness to play the fame game. His out-and-out success in *Casino Royale* saved him, but there will always be sections of the British press who are more than keen to dig the dirt on someone who won't jump through the publicity hoops. This is where the danger lies.

His early and brief marriage to actress Fiona Loudon and the existence of his daughter Ella from that marriage became public knowledge early in his career. But he won't discuss it, or his daughter, and woe betide the journalist who dares to ask.

He did confide in an *Observer* journalist in 2003 that he'd been trying to get his daughter to listen to The Rolling Stones but she was stuck on The Beatles . . . and that was as far as it went. And there was a brief mention of her at the time of Bond as he admitted: 'Ella's proud of me being James Bond, but I want to protect her. I don't bring her up in conversation much because the more I talk about her, the more the press have a right to take photos.'

His next relationship that was well documented was with German actress Heike Makatsch. Best known for her role as the marriage-wrecking secretary in *Love Actually*, Daniel had met her on the set of the movie *Obsession* in 1997. The relationship was to last seven years, and the pair were photographed publicly many times over this period.

He even told *The Times* in January 2004: 'I have to say I am in a very happy stage of my life. Whether we are going to get married I don't know. I think probably we'll end up being together, I hope for a long time, so we'll probably have to get married eventually.'

Sadly this wasn't to be as they split up a little later that same year. He then had a brief romance with supermodel Kate Moss, a liaison that brought the tabloids slavering to his door. This was a wake-up call for Daniel who had so far managed to evade the worst of invasive journalistic tactics. As he told women's magazine *Elle* later that year: 'All I'll say is, it was a lesson. They're like the secret service, the tabloids. You can be in the middle of

Caption: Daniel and Satsuki Mitchell arrive at the MTV Europe Music Awards 2006 in Copenhagen, Denmark.

nowhere and the mobile will go and it's so-and-so from whatever paper. They were at my mother's house in ten minutes. . . In the end, it was a relief because I've never chased that kind of celebrity, and it was confirmation that I didn't want it. And ninety-nine per cent of what they wrote was absolute shit.'

The relationship was brief and it was reported that Kate Moss was 'too wild' for Daniel. Her subsequent shenanigans with rocker Pete Doherty certainly lent validity to that theory. But as Daniel later said: 'If half the things they wrote about Kate and me actually happened it would have been

an interesting story – but they didn't.'

Daniel has avoided talking about any of his relationships and most of his ex's have been equally discreet. A woman with whom he went out when he was a student, Marina Pepper, has been the only one to step forward. And she was keen to stress his prowess in the bedroom. While he may have preferred this to remain private, it was hardly a shocking revelation.

When asked whether keeping his own counsel about his private life had proved more difficult since the Kate Moss affair, he was very definite in his response. 'I'd never talk about a previous relationship

Right: Marina Pepper, whom Daniel had known as a student, stepped forward with her 'kiss and tell' story.

Opposite: The rumours of an affair between Daniel and his *Layer Cake* co-star Sienna Miller were entirely unfounded.

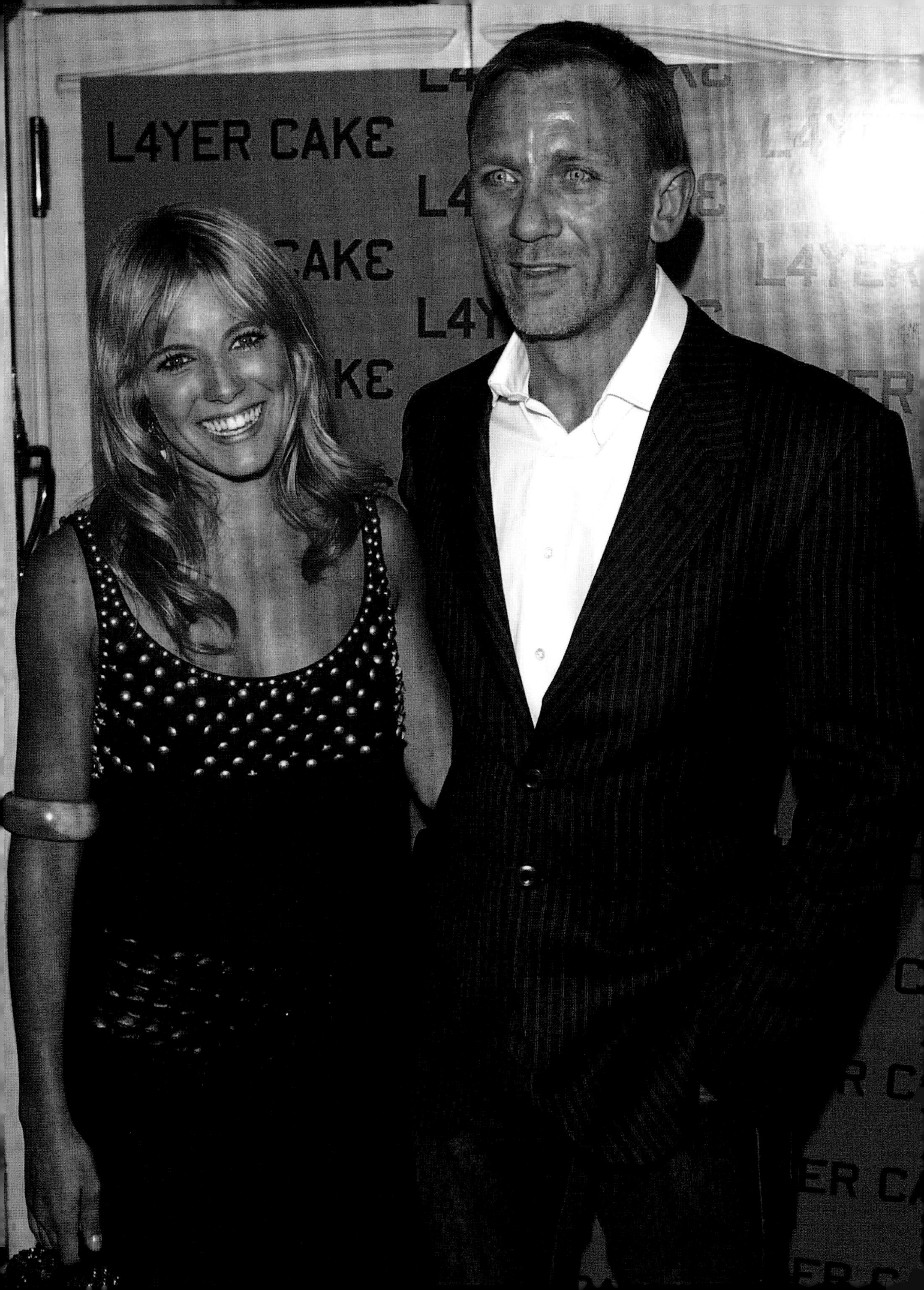
L4YER CAKE

even if it wasn't somebody famous and so I think the same rule has to be applied. The only reason I'd ever talk about that would be for my own advantage and that's really bad news. That's as low as you can go, as far as I'm concerned. If you're in a relationship with somebody – and we've all seen the relationships where they start battling it out in the press, God forbid that should ever happen – then you have to keep your own counsel. You have to. For your family, for your friends, for your children, whatever. Because only they should know what the truth is. Then they'll feel secure about themselves and if someone says to them, "He said this and blah blah," they'll be able to say, "I know the truth, you don't." That's the only way I can see it. That's the story, that's the way it goes.'

While he has always maintained a dignified silence over his relationships, he was to have to hide out to avoid the press in October 2005 when completely unfounded rumours of an alleged affair with young actress Sienna Miller broke. Both denied the affair, but it didn't stop it being splashed all over the front pages with the headline 'Sienna Cheats On Jude'.

Ironically, the story was deemed newsworthy not because of Daniel's fame but because Sienna was supposed to be in a relationship with fellow actor Jude Law. The Law-Miller relationship was widely reported in the press as an on-off romance, laying their private lives open to public scrutiny in exactly the way that Daniel was striving to avoid.

Both Daniel and Sienna Miller have consistently denied the claim that they were involved with one another, but that didn't stop the tabloids going to town. Yet nothing other than terse 'no comments' were issued, in keeping with Daniel's philosophy on not talking about his private life.

He was vehement in defence of this position in an *Arena* interview in 2006. When asked whether he felt himself to be tabloid fodder, he said: 'It's a question I can't answer. It seems I was tabloid fodder

Left: Daniel attends *The Golden Compass* premiere in London with Satsuki on his arm.

Opposite: Daniel has said of Satsuki, 'I couldn't get through it without her.'

Below: Playing an action hero and lothario on screen as '007' may have placed Daniel firmly in the public eye, but he remains an intensely private person.

if I was playing Bond or not anyway. But I really do believe that there is a huge imbalance as to what is considered to be private and what is public. I genuinely believe that it is a f***ing human right, no matter who you are or what you do, to have some privacy. I understand that you lose a bit of that when you do a job like this, but aspects of my life are nobody's f***ing business. Invasion of my privacy is something I will fight tooth and nail over. But I'm not going to start getting arsey about it because I'll lose. The papers have bigger bank balances than I do and I won't

get into a fight with them until I have to.'

Given that he once described self promotion as making him 'sick to his stomach' and has also likened it to going to the dentist, the already enormous burden of promoting the James Bond franchise must have seemed even greater. Perhaps the fact that he was in a stable relationship helped. He'd been dating American film producer Satsuki Mitchell since they met on the set of *The Jacket* in 2005.

They have made no secret of their relationship, having been pictured in public many times, and she accompanied

him to the premiere of *Casino Royale*. Talking about the strength he gains from their partnership, he managed to be both sweet and glowing. In an interview with *The Times* in November 2007 he said: 'I couldn't get through it without her. You've got to have a sense of perspective and she gives me that. It's a strain on a relationship because we are never in one place and there's never a lot of time. I have to fight for that, and for my family. It's a struggle, but I couldn't do it without having that closeness to somebody. Being on your own would be sad, sick and weird. I don't trust myself. I need that balance, it's crucially important. And we've been to some amazing places.'

Such amazing places included a private view of the Sistine Chapel, something not to forget in a hurry.

Daniel was particularly grateful that Satsuki was by his side during the madness of the Bond premiere. He also said that they'd decided together that she should be part of the whole Bond experience. 'The thing is, she's been with me all through this, and all the way through filming. So why exclude her? She's up to it; she's an adult, I'm an adult. I'm not going out there purposely holding her hand to say, "we're a couple". But Bond has been too big an experience, it might not come around again. We had to do that amazing thing in Leicester Square, and walk round all that craziness, just because it may never happen again.'

There have been rumours in the press about marriage between the pair, reports of glimpses of a big diamond ring. Despite the failure of his first marriage to Fiona Loudon, Daniel certainly hasn't ruled it out for a second time. When a journalist from the *Daily Telegraph* suggested to him back at the beginning of 2006 that he had difficulty with concepts such as marriage, Daniel admitted: 'Probably. I mean… probably, yes. I do believe in marriage, though. I really do. I do believe that getting together with somebody and making a public statement about it is a good thing. I just didn't really understand

that then. Whether or not I understand it more now is debatable, but commitment *is* a part of life. The toughest part, probably.'

As the Bond juggernaut rolls on with *The Quantum of Solace* and at least one other movie, he will constantly struggle to try to maintain that fine balance between public persona and private life. One sign that showed he was feeling the strain somewhat came with a report in the *Mirror* in April 2007. It was alleged that he'd sworn at a fan who'd tried to take a picture of him in famous London department store Harvey Nichols. 24-year-old Craig Evans alleged that Daniel had stormed over and sworn at him. He claimed that his day had been ruined and that he would never watch a James Bond film with Daniel in it again.

While he could probably afford to lose one fan, Daniel can't afford to lose his temper in public too often. There was also a report that he'd sworn at a Johann Hari, a journalist from *The Independent* when he'd jokingly asked him whether he was wearing the famous Bond trunks under his tuxedo at an awards ceremony.

Daniel has admitted that there are times when he needs to grit his teeth and smile. 'You know, if I'm up for it, fine. I have to keep hold of my sense of humour, because you can lose it very quickly and you start retreating into yourself; then you can't go anywhere unless you are with armed guards, and the whole thing becomes ridiculous. So you have to smile about these things. But I tell you, trying to take pictures of me when I'm having a piss is not welcome and never will be. And yes, that's happened.'

He's also aware that he's not a natural on the publicity circuit, as his rather awkward, less-than-relaxed performance at the initial Bond press conference bore out. Rather endearingly, he said that it was appearing on the *Parkinson* chat show that gave him the biggest problem.

'I was reluctant to go on *Parkinson* actually, which is weird because when it came to America I was like, "Oh fine, I'll do Letterman, I'll do whatever." I had less

fear about it because it's not my town. But suddenly you're at LWT in London and you're at the top of the f***ing stairs. The band's winking at you, and all you can think about is not falling down those stairs. Parkinson is delightful though, he came and talked to me before the show, and I thought: "OK, I don't have an act, this is all I can do, this is it, sorry." I admire people who can go and just turn it on. But if I do that, I just look like a wanker. So I try and talk normally with people.'

Perhaps the way forward in interviews is for him to be gently teased. Shameless BBC TV chat show host Jonathan Ross tried this and managed to raise a few smiles from a nervous Daniel. Having told him he was a 'very handsome man', he then went on to ruin it with, 'You've got a craggy old face. Kind of like a handsome Sid James.' Being compared to the long dead and far from gorgeous *Carry On* actor seemed to break the ice. For someone who had long ago decided he didn't want to go down the sex symbol route, it must have been a welcome relief.

Above: Unlike Robin Williams and Ben Elton, with whom he shared Parkinson's chat show set, Daniel felt he had no act to perform and simply had to be himself.

11

NOT ONLY SETTLING INTO BOND'S SHOES

When *Quantum Of Solace* was released in the UK on 31 October

2008, Daniel Craig sealed the deal as a very successful James

Bond indeed. A high-quality follow-up to the hugely popular *Casino*

Royale, *Quantum* picked up where that film had left off. Having been

betrayed by, then seen his lover Vesper Lynd killed, Bond is out for

revenge. As his boss M (Judi Dench) puts it so beautifully:

'I think you're so blinded by inconsolable rage,

you don't care who you hurt.'

As action-packed and gritty as the one that went before, *Quantum* added even more depth and colour to Daniel's radical reinterpretation of the British secret agent. Having signed up to the Bond adventure, it seemed he had embraced it with gusto.

In an on-set interview while filming *Quantum,* he confirmed his devotion to the role, telling a reporter: 'Until my joints go I will keep going as Bond. I have no intention of giving up just yet.'

Celebrating his 40th birthday during the making of the film, age and fitness were obviously on his mind, although he wasn't keen to discuss how he maintained his impressive physique: 'Bond used to do ten press ups and smoke 50 cigarettes and drink a bottle of something and pop a pill. So it doesn't sound very Bond-like to talk about fitness regimes.'

He described his character's state of mind in the film thus: 'At the end of *Casino Royale* the love of Bond's life has been taken from him. But Vesper Lynd

Right: As in *Casino Royale*, Daniel's *Quantum of Solace* 'Bond' was more casually dressed than previous incarnations of the character.

had also been forced to betray him and she has ripped him apart. That's where he's at. There is a sense of vengeance. He's out to get them.'

'Them' turn out to be the mysterious Quantum organisation, headed by the villainous Dominic Greene. He's played by Mathieu Amalric, a French actor who had co-starred with Daniel in Steven Spielberg's *Munich*. Mister Greene has a foul plot to exploit the world's water supplies, Bond is out to avenge his girl, and save the world as usual.

The physical routine was equally as battering as it had been on *Casino Royale*. The new Bond may have had emotional depths that we'd never witnessed before, but he was similarly adept in the fitness department. As Daniel explained: 'We are going from stunt sequence to stunt sequence. We did a body flight thing where you are free-falling in a wind tunnel. That was tough. I did a two-day fight sequence which we had been rehearsing for two months. That was physically very hard – getting hit, basically.'

Left: At times Daniel looked more like Steve McQueen in *The Great Escape* than a traditional 'Bond'.

There were more reports in the British press of physical damage sustained, too – the tip of one of his fingers apparently being sliced in an action sequence and a cut to his face that required eight stitches. A member of the Bond production team was quoted as saying: 'There was quite a lot of blood and it was decided he needed to go to hospital for emergency treatment.'

Other practical problems bedevilled the international production. Filming had to be suspended at the Presidential Palace in the Casca Viejo district of Panama when riots broke out in nearby Panama City. A representative of EON, the Bond production company said: 'We hope filming should be able to go ahead as normal from now on. None of the cast has been harmed.' Pictures did appear in the press, however, of Daniel surrounded by heavily armed guards.

The mayor of Chilean town Sierra Gorda also mounted a one-man protest by driving on to the set, apparently maddened that the Bond production team were passing off his town as being in neighbouring Bolivia. Carlos Lopez was arrested and charged with public disorder and trespassing. A spokeswoman for the producers simply said: 'Two policemen had to jump out of the way but fortunately nobody was injured. We have security on our sets and Daniel has security.'

While filming in Italy, a stuntman was seriously injured during a chase sequence as the Alfa Romeo he was driving crashed into a wall. This came just days after one of Bond's famous Aston Martins skidded into

Opposite: Daniel and Ukrainian actress Olga Kurylenko take a stroll in the desert in *Quantum of Solace*. Below: From the desert to the beach in *Flashbacks of a Fool*.

Lake Garda while being delivered to the set. It was later fished out of the lake.

Quantum was directed by Marc Forster who, having helmed both *Monsters' Ball* and *Finding Neverland*, was not known for his action movies. When asked if he was nervous about that, Daniel was adamant that it wasn't so. 'If we are going to do this, we have to create something that is going to last, that we are going to look to and say, "They were different". It's a risk, but the last one was a risk just because it was me getting involved, and we seem to have ridden that one out. So now we have to go to the next stage. I want to make sure the next two, three, four, whatever films I manage to do before they chuck me out, or before it goes tits up, sit nicely within this era.'

Having made the Bond role his own and clearly become very comfortable within the demanding franchise, Daniel was then free to make some other interesting choices. As he'd explained to his friend Sam Taylor Wood in an interview in *Interview* magazine: 'The criterion is, is it interesting? You often do jobs in response to what you've just done. If I've just played a crazy loon in one movie, I don't necessarily have the urge to go out and play another crazy loon for a while. I'm most likely not going to take any more spy roles in the foreseeable future. But then you never know – there might be something I can't pass up.'

His first 'interesting' choice was *Flashbacks Of A Fool*, released in the UK in April 2008. A low-budget, independent movie directed by his friend Baillie Walsh, it told the story of Joe Scott, a washed-up Hollywood movie star who returns to his home town for a friend's funeral. Daniel played Joe, a character that he would obviously hope to avoid becoming in real life. As he'd told *The Times* at the end of the preceding year: 'I mustn't get complacent because if I start relaxing about all of this, then I'm going to turn into a dick. I don't want to do that if I can possibly avoid it.'

He described the character and the film

thus: 'He's a washed up movie star. It's about going home and how some people run away from home not just because they're unhappy, but because that's what they're genetically predisposed to do. It's redemptive but not forgiving.

'Once you break those ties, they're gone. If you try to artificially reconnect them after twenty-five or however many years, it doesn't work, because friendships need constant work.'

Baillie Walsh was clearly delighted that Daniel, now an international movie star, had agreed to star in the film. 'Daniel liked the script and wanted to do the film – and he delivers a fantastic performance in the title role. Casting agents in Britain and America are falling over themselves to have him in their films. The fact that Daniel is still making films like mine when he could be earning ten times as much in Hollywood is a tribute to him.'

Flashbacks didn't set the box office alight but it satisfied Daniel's need to stay in touch with the independent movies on which he had built his career. As he once joked: 'If something comes along with a good script and it's shot with a torch and an Instamatic and set in a bike shed, then I'll do it.'

It also made him feel like an actor again, rather than an international superstar and he was happy that lending his name helped get the film made. 'I think we probably could have done it (pre-Bond) but it would have been harder and a struggle in a different way. It's not going to be a huge money-spinner because it's not that kind of movie. But to be able to make films like this is important to me. I have to be all these other things now and acting starts dropping down the list, which is bizarre. You go, "Hang on a minute, I just want to be an actor, I want to just turn up and do the gig."'

He was beginning to realise too that his new-found clout could be used to help others. As he told *The Independent* in April of 2008: 'I'm lucky enough to have met along the way some incredibly talented and lovely people. And I kind

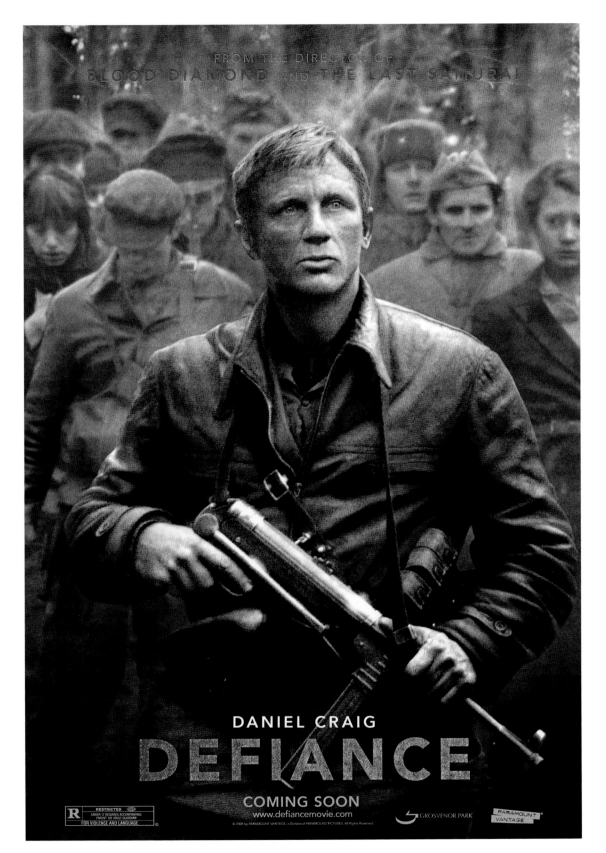

FROM THE DIRECTOR OF
BLOOD DIAMOND AND THE LAST SAMURAI

DANIEL CRAIG

DEFIANCE

COMING SOON
www.defiancemovie.com

GROSVENOR PARK

PARAMOUNT
VANTAGE

R RESTRICTED
UNDER 17 REQUIRES ACCOMPANYING
PARENT OR ADULT GUARDIAN
FOR VIOLENCE AND LANGUAGE

© 2008 by PARAMOUNT VANTAGE, a Division of PARAMOUNT PICTURES. All Rights Reserved.

Above: Jamie Bell, who starred in *Billy Elliot*, played Daniel's younger brother in *Defiance*.

Far right Far from being typecast as 'Bond', Daniel is now shooting for the stars.

of want to nurture them – or for them to help nurture me. When I was younger the idea of networking was a big luvvie joke, and on a basic level it's about self interest – there's nothing nice about it at all. But on a more generous level, it really is the sharing of information.'

His next choice was equally interesting and fitted very well into his pre-Bond CV of serious, quite often heavy, films. In *Defiance*, released on 4 January 2009, he played one of three Russian-Jewish brothers who go on the run in Nazi-occupied Belarus. The brothers rescue

members of their Jewish community, and lead them off to the forests where they live wild and gradually build a resistance movement, despite savage winter weather. Daniel played the part of "Tuvia Bielski", while Jamie Bell (of *Billy Elliot* fame) and Liev Schreiber, played the other two Bielski brothers.

The film, which had been shot on location in freezing cold Lithuania, pushed Daniel and everyone involved to the limits, as he told the BBC: "To keep warm we did a lot of drinking and I was wearing a little thermal on the sly but the

cold definitely had an effect. We were there 12 hours a day, six days a week and it got really cold, but there was something about that experience. Nobody did this for the money."

The weather wasn't the only challenge. Daniel and his fellow cast members also had to learn Russian – or at the very least a convincing Belarusian accent. Daniel ended up learning his lines phonetically in Russian, so that he could speak the words authentically, even if he didn't always fully understand what he was saying.

As *Defiance* was released, Daniel turned his attentions to theatre, as he prepared to make his Broadway debut in a play called *A Steady Rain*, about two Chicago police officers and their varying takes on episodes they have both experienced in the line of duty. The play opened at the end of September at the Gerald Schoenfeld Theatre in New York, with Daniel playing the part of "Joey" alongside Hugh Jackman (of *Wolverine* fame), playing "Denny", and enjoyed a successful run until 6 December.

As the year came to an end, Daniel took his theatre cap off and put his film hat back on, as he began preparations for a new film project called *Dream House*, which would see him star opposite old acquaintance Rachel Weisz. Little did he know at this time that working with the British actress would change the entire course of his personal life.

12

LOOKING AHEAD

2010 opened with Daniel consumed by shooting *Dream House*. Directed by Jim Sheridan, the film told the story of a family who move to their new dream house. However, the fantasy home turns out to be anything but, as the Atenton family are plagued by paranormal disturbances that appear to relate back to the previous owners: a family murdered under desperate circumstances.

Previous spread:
Daniel as Jake
Lonergan in
Cowboys & Aliens.
Below: Daniel with
future wife, actress
Rachel Weisz, in
Dream House.

For the film, Daniel was cast as Will Atenton, the father and husband of the family and Weisz was cast as his wife, Libby. In time, their playing husband and wife in the film would end up taking on a whole new meaning. Work on the film started in February on location in Canada, and lasted until April, when the shoot wrapped.

Dusting himself down from such a dark project, Daniel followed his usual scheme of polarising roles, by spending May getting ready to appear in Jon Favreau's *Cowboys & Aliens.* This new film, a genre mash-up as its title would suggest, told a story of aliens invading a small town in the Wild West in 1873. A mysterious stranger, Jake Lonergan, played by Daniel, initially threatens the town and its leader, Colonel Dolarhyde, played by Harrison Ford, but once the aliens arrive, he becomes the town's salvation.

Aside from getting to play cowboy all day and ride a horse on set (which true to his usual insistence on taking on as many

of his stunts as possible himself, Daniel mastered), Daniel was ecstatic to work with Harrison Ford, as he told *ScreenRant*: 'I'm a fan, and have been, as a lot of people are. But he's an actor and I've been lucky enough to find that when working with great actors that first and foremost all they want to do is to get it right.'

As with *Defiance*, Daniel had to adopt and perfect an accent. To authenticate his American accent, Daniel worked closely on set with a dialect coach. Their aim was to have Daniel's accent be convincing enough that audiences would notice he had adopted an American accent in his early scenes in the film and then promptly forget all about it. Daniel told the coach that he didn't want to lend the accent a distinctive Southern twang as he thought it would be both predictable and distracting.

Filming started in June 2010 and took place on location in New Mexico and California. The entire shoot lasted three months and finished in September.

In July, when Daniel was halfway through filming *Cowboys & Aliens*, it was

Below: Daniel in *Cowboys & Aliens*, acting alongside an actor he greatly admires, Harrison Ford.

Above: Daniel as Mikael Blomkvist in a scene from The *Girl With The Dragon Tattoo*, with young American actress, Rooney Mara.

Overleaf: Daniel as Mikael Blomkvist in the typically snowy landscape of *The Girl With The Dragon Tattoo*.

announced that he had signed up to play the lead role of Mikael Blomkvist, in an adaptation of the Swedish author Stieg Larsson's bestselling *Millenium* thriller trilogy. The first film, *The Girl with the Dragon Tattoo*, was to be directed by David Fincher and given Blomkvist's internalised, glacial persona, it made perfect sense to see Daniel take on the role.

With Rooney Mara, a young American actress who had sprung to overnight attention after her searing performance in the opening scenes of The Social Network cast as Lisbeth Salander, *The Girl with the Dragon Tattoo* started filming in September. Daniel and Mara travelled from location to location, as the film shot in Sweden, Norway, Switzerland, and on studio sets in California.

As a starting point for playing Mikael Blomkvist, Daniel did not watch the previous Swedish adaptations of the novels, so as not to fall under their influence. His preparation however, was child's play compared to Rooney Mara's. Even Daniel, who thought nothing of getting himself bruised or injured in pursuit of playing a character absolutely and authentically, was taken aback by the lengths Rooney Mara went to, in order to depict Lisbeth Salander as closely as possible to her character in Larsen's novels. Daniel later told *ShortList* that he was concerned for Mara, who as preparation for the role had lost weight, cut off her long hair, bleached her eyebrows and even pierced a nipple, her nose and an eyebrow to get into character: 'The poor girl was probably 91lbs when she was doing this movie because she was working out every day and dieting… she was waif-like because her character is that way, so she wasn't carrying an awful lot of fat to keep her warm. Her jeans had lots of rips in them and her costume was pretty thin. She really suffered.'

Towards the end of the shoot, news broke on TMZ that Rachel Weisz, Daniel's *Dream House* co-star had separated from her partner of nine years, the acclaimed filmmaker Darren Aronofsky. According to a news story that appeared on TMZ on 9 November: 'Reps for the former couple tell TMZ, "Rachel Weisz and Darren Aronofsky have been separated for some months. They remain close friends and are committed to raising their son together in NYC."'

The report went on to speculate about Weisz: 'Sources tell TMZ Rachel has been linked to James Bond star Daniel Craig for months. They worked together on the upcoming flick, *Dream House*, in February and March of 2010.' With no public comment from either Daniel or Weisz, the speculation failed to lift up out of rumour.

However, that speculation inched closer to fact when Daniel and Weisz were reported to have spent Christmas Day together. The *Daily Mail* claimed that the couple had been spotted over Christmas in Yeovil, Somerset, where they were believed to have rented a holiday cottage and been seen out having a drink in a local pub. The paper quoted an onlooker as saying: 'Daniel and Rachel looked like a romantic couple in a film. They were laughing and hanging on to each other's words and stopping to take photos of each other. They were clinging on to each other like honeymooners, the chemistry was obvious.' The report also mentioned that Daniel's relationship with Satsuki Mitchell had ended in November. Again, despite mounting speculation that they were indeed dating, neither Daniel nor Weisz either personally, or through their publicity channels, made any statement to either quash or affirm the rumours.

In January 2011, James Bond fans received a tonic in the form of an announcement that Bond 23, which had been on hold for financial reasons, would now go into production, with a projected November 2012 release attached to the project. Once more, Daniel would play James Bond.

Building on the Bond news, Daniel then appeared in a two minute film directed by the artist/filmmaker Sam Taylor Wood called *James Bond Supports International Women's Day*. The short, specially commissioned by EQUALS, a coalition of charities and organisations, was made to celebrate International Women's Day 2011. In the film, Daniel appears first as James Bond in one of his trademark slick suits and then in drag as a woman. Dame Judi Dench, offered her voice as M. After premiering on 8 March for International Women's Day at the Birds Eye View Film Festival at the BFI Southbank, Taylor Wood's film was then shown in cinemas and online, promoting awareness about issues of gender equality to a mainstream audience.

In May 2011, Daniel saw the release of his contribution to another short film: this one made by the British art duo, the Chapman Brothers. In the 15 minute short *The Organ Grinder's Monkey*, which starred Rhys Ifans, Daniel played Bubbles, alongside a cast which also included Thandie Newton, Rosamund Pike and Kevin Spacey.

As the summer came on, on 22 June 2011, Daniel put a stop to all the rumours by marrying Rachel Weisz in a tiny, private wedding ceremony in New York, attended only by Daniel's daughter, Ella; Henry Chance, the son Weisz has with former partner, Darren Aronofsky; and two family friends. The ceremony was kept tightly under wraps and details were not released to the public. That they married so soon after they started dating, was testimony to how intensely and quickly they had fallen in love.

When *Cowboys & Aliens* was released on 31 July, the film failed to excite critics – or audiences for that matter – and Favreau's ambitious, genre-bending, would-be

Above: Happy times
for Daniel and Rachel
Weisz, who quietly
married in 2011.

summer blockbuster ended up not doing as well as hoped. As to be expected, while promoting the film, Daniel had to bat away questions about his marriage to Weisz, since they were now an A-list Hollywood celebrity couple. At a press junket, Daniel told reporters that he and Weisz had deliberately planned it as a secret wedding and that they had no intention of revealing the details of the day: 'I did it secretly – I can't tell you how I pulled it off. My private life is incredibly important to me.'

Hot on the heels of *Cowboys & Aliens*, *Dream House* was released on 30 September 2011. Critics panned the film and it turned out to be a commercial flop. Despite this, audiences were drawn to the film to see Daniel and Rachel Weisz playing husband and wife, *before* they became husband and wife in real life – in search of signs of budding chemistry between the old acquaintances. The fact that neither Daniel nor Weisz still had not shed any light on

how or when they fell for each other, only added to the intrigue.

Meanwhile, as positive advance buzz grew around *The Girl with the Dragon Tattoo*, Daniel stepped once more into the shoes of James Bond. With Sam Mendes in the director's chair, Bond 23 started filming in November. In this latest Bond saga, M comes under threat and it is up to Bond to investigate the threat and resolve it.

The shoot would last until May 2012 and take in locations in Turkey and across the UK, with a significant number of scenes shot in and around London. Daniel, as always, threw himself fully into the role, as he later told *Empire* magazine: 'When I'm doing the movie I'm totally single-minded. I keep my energy levels as high as I can all the time. I want to inspire, and be inspired.'

A month into the shoot, on 20 December, *The Girl with the Dragon Tattoo* was released. In stark contrast to the lukewarm

critical reactions to *Cowboys & Aliens* and *Dream House*, this film earned Fincher, Daniel and Mara, strong reviews and a potent turnout at the box office.

Putting the icing on the prolific output of the second half of 2011, Steven Spielberg's technologically dazzling animated film, *The Adventures of Tintin: The Secret of the Unicorn*, was released on 21 December 2011, featuring Daniel's voice for the part of Sakharine/Red Rackham.

The first half of 2012 rushed by in a frantic blur, with Daniel busy either promoting *The Girl with the Dragon Tattoo*, or working on Bond 23, which was now known by its official title, *Skyfall*. By the time he finished shooting *Skyfall* in May, he was understandably eager to take time off.

On 27 July, sticking with the Bond theme, Daniel wowed global audiences by bringing a winning promotional moment for *Skyfall* to life, in the form of a short, satirical Bond film, which was screened towards the end of Danny Boyle's Opening Ceremony for the 2012 London Olympics. The short film saw Daniel arrive in character as Bond at Buckingham Palace, walk down a long corridor and arrive at the office of the real-life Queen Elizabeth II. After greeting one another – a timeless moment – they are next seen in a helicopter, flying past a variety of well-known London sights. Then, the Queen, showing a flash of surprising willingness and humour, appeared to leap from the helicopter and parachute down into the Olympic stadium. Daniel took the event in his stride, and said he was genuinely surprised to find himself in a room with the Queen, as he had anticipated that particular day to be a day off from work. After the ceremony it was revealed that this short Bond film had been shot back in April and kept fiercely under wraps.

After so much silence on the subject, Daniel's fans were excited to read Rachel Weisz open up about her marriage to

Above: Daniel's star turn as James Bond acting opposite Queen Elizabeth II for the London 2012 Olympics Opening Ceremony.
Overleaf: Daniel as James Bond in *Skyfall* during the epic motorcycle scene set in the Grand Bazaar of Istanbul.

Daniel in an interview with *Hello*, published in August. She told the magazine, 'I love being married to Daniel. It's a wonderful feeling of stability and it's very grounding. I mean, it hasn't made me more domestic or anything – just being married doesn't suddenly make you able to cook – but I am very happy right now. Extremely happy, in fact.'

In September, it was announced that Daniel had signed up for two further Bond films, known at this stage as Bond 24 and Bond 25. This announcement made Daniel the third most-cast as Bond actor after Sean Connery and Roger Moore. In the spiralling association between Daniel and the character of James Bond, it seemed that he was being firmly branded as the definitive James Bond of this era. News reports stated that Daniel had signed a £31 million deal for the two films – a massive

jump from the £1.9 million deal for playing Bond in *Casino Royale*.

Powered by very positive reviews, when *Skyfall* was released on 9 November 2012, it turned out to be a massive critical and commercial success. The film went on to gross a staggering $1 billion worldwide.

Moving into 2013, Daniel was immersed in promoting the film and as he did so, Hollywood's rumour mill went wild speculating as to his next move. Would he make *The Girl Who Played with Fire* next? Or Bond 24? As the screenplays to both films sped ahead, Daniel enjoyed turning 45 on 12 March, as he took delivery of an Aston Martin V12 Vantage car. Several weeks later, as follow-up to his pre-Olympics royal encounter, he and Rachel were invited to Windsor Castle, to dine with the Queen, in the company of select guests from the worlds of film, theatre and TV,

Below: Bond in a tight spot with Silva, played by Spanish actor Javier Bardem.
Opposite: The critical and commercial success of *Skyfall* proved that Daniel had been accepted as this generation's definitive James Bond.

including actress Helena Bonham Carter and her filmmaker partner, Tim Burton.

At this time in his life, with three successful Bond movies under his belt, and two further Bond films in the pipeline, not to mention the forthcoming second and third instalments of Stieg Larsson's *Millenium* series, a happily-married Daniel finds himself in a position that other actors would find utterly enviable.

He has managed to take on the famous, yet precarious, role of James Bond without compromising a dot of his integrity, and with that and other concurrent roles, notably *The Girl with the Dragon Tattoo*, his career has risen up to a level where he can now afford comfortably to pick and choose the parts that speak to him.

With so many high profile roles in the pipeline, there's no doubt we'll be seeing a lot more of Daniel in the decades to come and whatever choices he makes, they'll no doubt be both contrary and challenging. So at this point, with such a stunning record of success behind him, what keeps driving him? 'I'm definitely not satisfied about my career. I don't know how you can be; it's the very nature of things. I'm always trying to figure it out and I'm kind of unsatisfied constantly. I always want to get it right and I don't know what The Answer to it is. But I do know that it's out there and I do know it's worth looking for.'

Left: Daniel stands loyally beside M, played by Judi Dench, in *Skyfall*.

PICTURE CREDITS